Other books in the NIrV Kid Reference Library

Kidcordance
Kidatlas

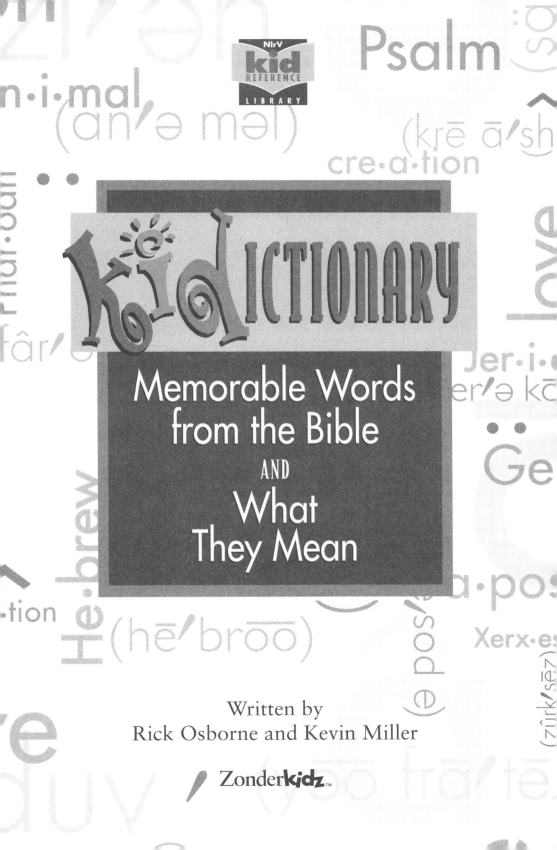

Kidictionary

Memorable Words from the Bible
AND
What They Mean

Written by
Rick Osborne and Kevin Miller

Zonderkidz™

Zonder**kidz**™

The children's group of Zondervan

www.zonderkidz.com

Kidictionary
Copyright 2002 by Lightwave Publishing Inc.

Requests for information should be addressed to:

Grand Rapids, Michigan 49530

ISBN: 0–310–70077–9

LIGHT w a v e
building Christian faith in families

A Lightwave Production
P.O. Box 160 Maple Ridge
B.C., Canada V2X 7G1

www.lightwavepublishing.com

Editor: Barbara J. Scott
Cover and interior design: Lori Vezina
Art direction: Jody Langley

Printed in the United States of America

02 03 04 05 /❖DC/ 5 4 3 2 1

Abba (*ab*-ah)
Not to be confused with the popular 1970s rock group, Abba is Aramaic for "daddy" or "papa." In Jesus' time, Abba was what children called their fathers. Jesus used this word when he prayed to show his disciples that God loved them like a father loved his children.

Abednego (ah-*bed*-ne-go)
The Babylonian name of Azariah, one of Daniel's friends. Daniel and his three friends were educated in the language and culture of the Babylonians while they were prisoners in Babylon. Abednego, Shadrach, and Meschach were chucked into a furnace for refusing to worship Nebuchadnezzar's golden statue, but no sweat! — God miraculously rescued them (Daniel 3).

Abel (*ay*-bel)
The second son of Adam and Eve. Abel was a shepherd. His brother Cain was so jealous that God accepted Abel's offering and not his, that he killed Abel (Genesis 4:4–5, 8). Cain should've clued in: God accepted Abel's offering only because he offered a blood sacrifice — something Cain hadn't done.

Abijah/Abijam (a-*buy*-jah/a-*buy*-jam)
The second king of Judah and son of Rehoboam. Abijah (also called Abijam) tried to reason with the northern kingdom. He pleaded with them, "Don't mess with us. God is on our side," but they treacherously attacked anyway. *Big* mistake. God helped Abijah pound them into the dust.

Abimelech (ah-*bim*-eh-lek)
1. The king of Gerar during Abraham's time. 2. One of Gideon's sons, the in-law (actually, *outlaw*) who murdered all seventy of his brothers, except *one!* Abimelech's evil life was finally brought to an end in Thebez, when a woman with good aim dropped a millstone on his head. *Ouch!*

Abner (*ab*-ner)
Saul's top military commander. After Saul's death, Abner helped set up Saul's son Ishbosheth as king instead of David. But Abner and Ishbosheth eventually had a falling out, so Abner joined up with David instead. Problem was, Abner had killed the brother of Joab, David's military commander. So when Abner showed up, Joab killed *him*.

Abraham
(*a*-bra-ham)

God changed Abram's name to Abraham and promised to turn his descendants into a great nation (Genesis 12:1–3). Abraham's first reaction was "Come again?" (rough translation), because he and his wife Sarah didn't have any children—and they were *way* too old to start! But Abraham believed God, and God kept his promise by giving Abraham and Sarah a son, Isaac. That's why Abraham is called the father of all who have faith (Romans 4:16).

Absalom (*ab*-sa-lom)
Absalom was known for his good looks and beautiful hair and was David's favorite son. However, he revolted against his father and crowned himself king. Absalom's rebellion came to a sad end when he caught his head in a tree branch as he was fleeing David's army. Joab, David's military commander, found him hanging there and, well, finished him off.

abyss (ah-*biss*)
1. The ocean or a deep mass of water (Genesis 1:2). 2. A bottomless pit. 3. A prison where demons and evil spirits are punished. The demons were terrified that Jesus might send them there and begged him not to do it (see Luke 8:31). You can bet they would've screamed all the way down!

Achaia (a-*kay*-a)
The name the Romans gave to the southern part of Greece when they captured Corinth in 146 B.C. The two major cities of Achaia were Athens and Corinth, and Paul witnessed in both places. In Corinth, the Jewish leaders accused Paul of breaking their laws, but Gallio, the governor of Achaia, threw the bums out (see Acts 18:1–17; 19:21).

Achan (*ay*-kan)
An Israelite who lived up to his name: "troublemaker." Before the Israelites conquered Jericho, God told them not to take any booty. But Achan had sticky

fingers and snagged some stuff. The result? Achan and his family were stoned, and Israel got its butt kicked in the next battle. Lesson learned.

Adam and Eve (a-dum and eev)
The first people God created (Genesis 2:7, 21–22). Adam was formed from the dust, and Eve was created from one of Adam's ribs. (Pretty creative stuff!) Adam and Eve lived happily in the Garden of Eden, but not happily ever after. One day Satan tempted Eve to eat a forbidden fruit. She convinced Adam to do the same, and they both wound up out of the garden and separated from God. We've been choking on that fruit ever since.

adultery (a-*dull*-ter-ee)
When a married person has a sexual relationship with someone who is not that person's spouse. Adultery is serious business, because it ruins families, communities, even nations! That's why in the Old Testament, the penalty for adultery was death (Leviticus 20:10). Jesus said that even looking at someone lustfully is considered adultery (Matthew 5:28). So don't even think about it!

Agabus (*ag*-a-bus)
A prophet from Jerusalem who predicted severe famine throughout the Roman world (Acts 11:28). Later Agabus tied himself with Paul's belt to show that Paul would be bound by his enemies and handed over to the Romans. Let's just say that when you saw this guy, you didn't bother asking him for the *good* news.

Agag (*ay*-gag)
1. A common name for the Amalekite kings. 2. The king of the Amalekites who was spared by Saul contrary to God's wishes (1 Samuel 15:8–33). Agag couldn't believe his good fortune, but it didn't last long. When Samuel found out what happened, he had Agag cut into pieces.

Ahab (*ay*-hab)
The seventh king of Israel. Ahab could have been a good king, but he let his evil wife Jezebel run his life. First she convinced him that Baal should be worshiped along with God. Then she had him kill God's priests. Maybe he should have let his parents choose his wife for him!

Ahaz (*ay*-haz)
The eleventh king of Judah. He was such an evil, shifty character that when he died, he wasn't even given a proper burial (2 Chronicles 28:27). Ahaz is remembered for almost single-handedly destroying Judah by trusting in Assyria instead of God. God punished him by letting other countries invade Judah.

altar (*all*-ter)
A table made of stones or metal on which priests offered sacrifices to God. The Hebrew word for altar means "a place of slaughter or sacrifice." In the Old Testament, altars were also used to remind the Israelites of their past or to call attention to major events (Genesis 8:20).

Alexandria (al-ex-*and*-ree-ah)
The capital of Egypt during Greek and Roman times. It was named after the Greek conqueror Alexander the Great who established the city when he conquered Egypt in 331 B.C. Alexandria soon became one of the most important cultural and intellectual centers in the Mediterranean.

alien (*ale*-ee-un)
Contrary to what you may read in the *National Enquirer* (You don't read that stuff, do you?) aliens during Bible times were not creatures who showed up in flying saucers and said, "Take me to your leader." An alien was simply a foreigner, someone from a country other than Israel.

Alpha and Omega (*al*-fa and o-*meg*-ah)
1. The first and last letters in the Greek alphabet.
2. The name used by God the Father and God the Son (Jesus). This name shows that God is the Creator and the final Judge of all creation (Revelation 1:8; 22:13).

Amalek (*am*-ah-lek)
The son of Esau's eldest son Eliphaz. He was the chieftain of an Edomite tribe. Scholars disagree about whether or not this tribe eventually became known as the Amalekites, because the Amalekites were around long before Amalek was born (Genesis 14:7).

Amalekites (a-*mal*-eh-kites)
A wandering tribe that lived in the deserts south of the area that became Israel. They were one of Israel's most bitter enemies throughout the Old Testament. They kept attacking Israel, but without much success. They were defeated by Kedor-laomer, Joshua, Gideon, Saul, David, and the Simeonites. That's zero for six.

Amen (a-*men*)
The word that Christians and Jews use to end their prayers. It means, "May it be so." By saying "Amen," we are saying we trust God and know he has heard our prayers. Christians also say "Amen" to agree with what someone else is saying, as in "Amen! Preach it, brother!"

Ammon (*am*-mun)
1. The son of Lot who became the father (ancestor) of the people of Ammon (Genesis 19:38). 2. The land settled by Lot's descendants, the Ammonites, located northeast of the Dead Sea.

Ammonites (*am*-mun-ites)
The descendants of Lot's son Ammon. The Ammonites were enemies with Israel for most of their history. They were among the armies who fought against King (Jumpin') Jehoshaphat and wound up slaughtering each other when God caused confusion among them (2 Chronicles 20:1–23).

Amorites (*am*-oh-rites)
A large group of people who lived west of the Euphrates River. Their name means "westerners" or "tall ones." Israel often clashed with the Amorites. Like the Canaanites, the Amorites were first settled in the Promised Land. When the Amorites were finally defeated, they became Israel's servants (1 Kings 9:19–21).

Amos (*a*-mus)
One of the twelve minor prophets. Amos was formerly a shepherd and a fig picker from Judah. God called him to prophesy to Israel during the reign of Uzziah, king of Judah, and Jeroboam, king of Israel. Amos's prophecies are recorded in (no surprise) the book of Amos.

Ananias (an-ah-*ni*-us)
1. A member of the Jerusalem church who, along with his wife Sapphira, tried to trick the church concerning the amount of their offering. He fell over dead as a result (Acts 5:1–5). 2. A Christian from Damascus who was sent by God to help the apostle Paul after he was struck blind (Acts 9:10–19). 3. The high priest before whom Paul appeared before being sent to Felix. He ordered some men to strike Paul on the mouth, and Paul responded by calling him a "pretender," quite an insult in those days. Paul apologized when he realized who Ananias was (Acts 23:2–5).

Andrew (*an*-drew)
One of Jesus' first disciples. Andrew was originally a disciple of John the Baptist and started following Jesus once John said Jesus was the Messiah. Andrew introduced his brother Simon Peter to Jesus, and he became a disciple as well. According to tradition, Andrew was crucified on an X-shaped cross in Greece.

angel (*ane*-gel)
Powerful spiritual beings created by God before the beginning of the world (Job 38:4–7). Angels serve God by delivering messages, protecting people from

harm, helping people escape, feeding them, and even fighting battles for them. Note: The Bible doesn't say that angels have wings or halos! See *cherubim*.

anger (*ang*-er)
A strong feeling of displeasure. Anger is often thought of as a bad thing, but it's okay to get angry about some things, like when others are being mistreated. However, flying off the handle will only get you into trouble. It won't make you very popular either.

anoint (ah-*noint*)
To pour oil on someone to set that person apart for a special job. God anointed people to be kings, priests, or prophets. In the New Testament, people were anointed by the Holy Spirit to do God's work. If you're a Christian, you're anointed!

Antichrist, the
(*an*-tee-krist)
The ultimate bad guy — the archenemy of God on earth. According to John, he will rise up before the second coming of Christ and, with the help of his false prophet, will trick people into worshiping him instead of Jesus (Revelation 13:11–12). The Antichrist had better take some swimming lessons, because he's going to spend eternity in a lake of fire (Revelation 19:20).

Antioch (*an*-tee-awk)
1. Capital of the Roman province of Syria and an important commercial city on the Mediterranean. Following Stephen's death, many Christians escaped persecution in Jerusalem by fleeing to Antioch, and it soon became a major Christian center. 2. Pisidian Antioch was a city in central Turkey where Paul established a church (Acts 13:14–49).

Apollos (a-*pol*-loss)
A leader in the early church and a friend of the apostle Paul. Apollos was born in Alexandria and knew the Old Testament Scriptures super well. When Priscilla and Aquila heard him preach in Ephesus, they knew this guy was a winner. He just needed to know more about Jesus. From Ephesus, Apollos went to Corinth, where he was so popular that he accidentally caused a split in the church (1 Corinthians 1:11–13; 3:1–8).

apostle (ah-*poss*-ull)
A special messenger of God, particularly one of the twelve men Jesus chose to start his church (Luke 6:13). The apostles learned from Jesus, then went out to preach, heal people, and drive out demons. Almost every one of Jesus' apostles was eventually martyred. Talk about dedication! See *disciple*.

Aquila (ah-*kwil*-ah)
A Jewish tentmaker and believer from Rome who had moved to Corinth. He and his wife Priscilla sewed tents with Paul when he came to Corinth. Then they accompanied Paul on his journey until they reached Ephesus. There they met Apollos and taught him more about Christ.

Arabia (ah-*ray*-bee-ah)
A desert region between the Red Sea and the Persian Gulf, which today makes up the Sinai Peninsula and Saudi Arabia. The Queen of Sheba came from southern Arabia to pay Solomon a visit (1 Kings 10:1–13). Paul also holed up in Arabia for a couple of years (Galatians 1:17).

Aram (*ah*-ram)
A son of Shem and ancestor of the Arameans. The Arameans lived in what is now modern Syria. David conquered Aram, including Damascus, their capital (see 2 Samuel 8, 10). Later Aram broke free (1 Kings 11:23–24) and became a major threat to the Israelites. Aram often attacked the northern kingdom of Israel.

Aramaic (air-a-*may*-ik)
The language of Aram (Syria), spoken by many people during Bible times. Parts of the Old Testament were written in Aramaic. The New Testament also contains a sprinkling of Aramaic words among the Greek. Many of Jesus' teachings were spoken in Aramaic and then translated into Greek for the Gospels.

Ararat (*air*-ah-rat)
A mountain range located between the Black Sea and the Caspian Sea where Noah's ark landed after the Flood. Later the name Ararat was used for that one famous mountain in the range. Many people think Noah's ark is still on Mount Ararat, but its site has not been positively identified.

Ark of the Covenant (*cov*-eh-nent)
A beautiful, gold-covered, wooden chest that contained the original Ten Commandments and other religious items. The ark symbolized the presence of God to the Israelites, and they often carried it into battle (Joshua 6:3–16). The ark disappeared when Nebuchadnezzar's armies destroyed Jerusalem in 586 B.C. Indiana Jones found it in the movies, but we're still looking.

ark, Noah's

A huge ship that Noah built (following God's blue-prints) to save his family and two of every kind of clean animal from the Flood. The ark was *huge*, almost one hundred feet longer than a foot-ball field and taller than a three-story building. It took 120 years to build!

Armageddon
(ar-mah-*ged*-don)

The Greek name for a valley located between Mount Carmel and Jezreel. Armageddon was the crossroads for two important trade routes and the site of many major battles. In the last days, the Battle of Armageddon will be fought between God and the armies of Satan (Revelation 16:16).

armor (*are*-mur)

Protective metal or leather clothing worn by soldiers going into battle. Armor in Bible times wasn't anything like what knights wore in the Middle Ages. All soldiers wore was a shield, a helmet, a breastplate, greaves (shin guards), and a girdle. Don't laugh. This type of girdle didn't suck in your belly; it protected it!

armor of God (*are*-mur)

The qualities Christians need in order to protect themselves while they do battle for God (Ephesians 6:10–18). The armor includes the belt of truth, the breast-plate of righteousness, the shield of faith, the helmet of salvation, and the sword of the Spirit. Do you have your armor on?

army (*ar*-mee)

A group of soldiers organized and trained for war. Unlike most of its neighbors, Israel didn't have an army until the time of Saul and David. Before that, they banded together with their farm tools to fight off their enemies — or trusted God to do their fighting for them.

Asa (*ay*-sah)

Third king of Judah and son of Abijah. Asa started out well. He worked hard to get rid of the idols and bring his people back to God. But later he depended on God less and less. The result? He died (2 Chronicles 16:7–10, 12).

Ascension, the.
See *Jesus going to heaven.* (Ah-*sen*-shun)

Asher (*ash*-er)
Jacob's eighth son and father of one of the twelve tribes of Israel. Little is known about Asher except that his people were possibly good cooks (Genesis 49:20). His descendants received land in northern Israel. They never did manage to kick the Phoenicians out like they were supposed to.

Asherah (*ash*-er-rah)
A goddess of the Canaanites and wife of the false god Baal. People carved Asherah's image on wooden poles, stuck them in the ground, then bowed down in the shavings and worshiped the pole. *Dumb!* Worship of Asherah was a real stumbling block for the ancient Israelites.

Asia (*ay*-zhuh)
A Roman province in what is now western Turkey. God stopped the apostle Paul from preaching in Asia on his second missionary journey. Later on Paul preached up a storm in Ephesus (a major Asian city) for two years so that all the Jews and Greeks who lived in Asia could hear the word of the Lord (Acts 19:10).

Assyria/Assyrians (ah-*seer*-ee-ah)
An empire to the northeast of Israel, where Syria and Iraq are now. The Assyrians were like the bully on the block—a cruel, warlike people who went out each year and fought other nations to get money and slaves to build their cities. They conquered northern Israel in 722 B.C.

astrology (ah-*strawl*-oh-gee)
The study of the sun, moon, planets, and stars and how their movements affect human behavior and predict future events. The Bible forbids astrology (and any other way of predicting the future) not only because it doesn't work but also because it leads people into the occult and away from God (1 Samuel 15:23; 28:3–25).

Athens (*a*-thenz)
The capital of southern Greece and the intellectual center of the ancient world. On his second missionary journey, Paul stopped in Athens to wait for Timothy and Silas. He was shocked by all the idols in the city, so he preached the gospel on Mars' Hill, an important building in Athens (Acts 17:16–34). (The map on the following page shows where you can find the city of Athens.)

Augustus Caesar *(uh-gust-us see-zer)*

The title given to Octavian (63 B.C.–A.D. 14), the first Roman emperor, and all emperors after him. For example, the Caesar mentioned in Acts 25:21, 25 is not Octavian but Nero (A.D. 37–A.D. 68), the fifth emperor of Rome. Christ was born during Octavian's reign, which lasted forty-four years.

Baal *(bay-ul)*

The chief Canaanite god. The Canaanites believed Baal controlled the rain, so they worked hard to keep him happy. (They had their own rain dance too.) However, when God *kept* it from raining and sent down fire, it proved Baal was nothing but a figment of the Canaanites' imagination (1 Kings 17:1; 18:24, 38).

Babel *(ba-bull)*

A city in southern Babylonia with an enormous tower. Babel was built after the Flood by proud people who were trying to make a name for themselves. God punished them by confusing their language and scattering them across the earth like so much chicken feed (Genesis 11:1–9).

Babylon (*bab*-i-lawn)

A city located along the Euphrates River in what is modern-day Iraq. Babylon was founded by Nimrod, grandson of Noah's son Ham. Much later, Babylon was the capital of the huge Babylonian empire that became Judah's enemy. The book of Revelation symbolically describes an evil world government as "Babylon the Great" (Revelation 14:8).

Balaam (*bay*-lam)

A magician hired by Balak, the Moabite king, to curse the Israelites before they entered Canaan. However, after finding out he wasn't even as smart as his donkey (whom God allowed to speak), Balaam finally listened to God and wound up blessing the Israelites instead (Numbers 22–24).

baptism
(*bap*-tism)

A ceremony that identifies us with Jesus. Jesus commanded all Christians to be baptized as a sign that he has forgiven our sins. Baptism can be done in many ways, often by dunking someone under water. (But not in a dunk tank!) However your church baptizes, baptism's an important event for every Christian.

Barabbas (bar-*ab*-bus)

The prisoner who was released by Pilate at the Passover Feast. Jesus was innocent, but Barabbas was a criminal who deserved to be in prison. (He was in jail for rebellion and murder.) The religious leaders were so bent on having Jesus killed they didn't care who was released instead of him.

Barak (*bay*-rak)

Deborah, a prophetess and judge, asked Barak to assemble an army of ten thousand men to fight the Canaanites. Barak agreed to do it only if Deborah would march into battle with him. She agreed, and with the help of a little storm God whipped up, they whupped the Canaanites'.

Barnabas (*bar*-na-bus)
His original name was Joseph, but Jesus' disciples renamed him Barnabas (Son of Encouragement). Barnabas convinced the Christians in Jerusalem that Saul (Paul) really had become a Christian. Then Barnabas helped Paul escape to Tarsus when his religious enemies in Jerusalem tried to kill him. Later Barnabas went with Paul on a missionary journey.

Bartholomew (bar-*thol*-uh-mew)
One of Jesus' twelve disciples. In the gospel of John, he is called Nathaniel. He is most famous for saying, "Nazareth! Can anything good come from there?" (John 1:46). Yes! *Jesus* came from Nazareth. Tradition says Bartholomew preached the gospel in Armenia and India before being crucified upside down.

Baruch (bar-*ruke*)
Baruch was a professional scribe (like a secretary) and one of the closest, most loyal friends of the prophet Jeremiah. Baruch wrote down all the prophecies Jeremiah spoke and then read them to the people and royal officials. Sometimes this got him and Jeremiah in *big* trouble.

Bathsheba (bath-*shee*-ba)
The wife of Uriah and later of King David. David committed adultery with Bathsheba after he noticed her bathing. When he discovered she was pregnant, David tried to trick Uriah into thinking it was his child. When this failed, David had Uriah killed, then took Bathsheba as his wife. They had four children together, including Solomon.

battle (*ba*-tul)
A fight between two armies. Throughout its history, Israel was involved in many battles. There were battles when they took over the Promised Land and more battles when they defended it from attackers. Battles were so common in Old Testament times that spring was called "the time when kings go off to war" (2 Samuel 11:1). Can you imagine living in that kind of world?

Beast, the (beest)
The ultimate bad guy, the archenemy of God on earth, also known as the Antichrist. According to John, the Beast will rise up before the second coming of Christ and, with the help of his false prophet (who is also called a beast), will trick people into worshiping him instead of God (Revelation 13:11–12). But the Antichrist and his little beast buddy had better take some swimming lessons, because he's going to spend eternity in a lake of fire (Revelation 19:20).

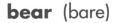

bear (bare)

A large, hairy mammal. You don't find bears in Israel anymore, but during Old Testament times, they were a constant threat. David killed a bear with his — ahem — bare hands to protect his sheep (1 Samuel 17:34–35). Bears are also used in the Bible to describe people who are cunning or fierce.

Beatitudes, the. See *Blessings, the.* (bee-at-i-tudes)

Beelzebub (bee-*el*-zee-bub)

Another name for the Devil or Satan. Some people think the word is a version of the word *beelzebul,* which literally means "dung god." Others think the word comes from *baal-zebub,* which was the Philistine "god of flies." Either way, he was one smelly guy!

Beersheba (beer-*shee*-bah)

A city halfway between the Mediterranean Sea and the southern tip of the Dead Sea. It was near there that God spoke to Hagar (Genesis 21:17), Isaac (Genesis 26:23–33), and Jacob (Genesis 46:1–5). Beersheba was also the place where Esau sold his birthright to Jacob and where Elijah fled from Jezebel.

believe (buh-*leeve*)

To accept something as true. Believing in something is different from simply knowing that it's true. Believing means acting on what you know. For example, it's not enough to *know* that Jesus is God. (James 2:19 says even the demons know that!) You have to *act* on that knowledge by accepting Jesus as your Savior.

Belshazzar (bell-*sha*-zar)

Last ruler and party animal of the Babylonian Empire. Belshazzar's fun came to a sudden end one night when a mysterious hand appeared and started writing on the wall. He called Daniel to interpret the writing and discovered it was a message of doom for him and his kingdom. Belshazzar died that very night (Daniel 5).

Benjamin (*ben*-ja-min)

Jacob's youngest son, who became the great-great-great-granddaddy of the tribe of Benjamin, one of the twelve tribes of Israel. Jacob's favorite wife, Rachel, had two sons: Joseph and Benjamin. After Rachel died (and it looked like Joseph had too), Jacob was very attached to Benjamin.

Berea (beh-*ree*-ah)

A city in northern Greece where the apostle Paul stopped on his second missionary journey. Paul really admired the people of Berea because they dug into the Scriptures to make sure that what he was telling them was true (Acts 17:11).

Bethany (*beth*-an-ee)

A village located two miles from Jerusalem on the road to Jericho. Bethany was an important place in Jesus' life. It was here that he raised Lazarus from the dead (John 11) and was anointed with perfume by Mary. Jesus also spent a night in Bethany the week before his crucifixion.

Bethel (*beth*-el)

This city's name means "house of God." Located twelve miles north of Jerusalem, it was where Jacob had his vision of a stairway going from earth to heaven (Genesis 28:12). Bethel was also a temporary resting place for the Ark of the Covenant. In later years, Bethel became a center for idol worship.

Bethlehem (*beth*-le-hem)

A town located just a few miles south of Jerusalem. It is famous for a lot of reasons. First, it was the town Ruth moved to when she left Moab. Second, it was where King David was born. Finally, and most importantly, it was the birthplace of Jesus. Hey! Who says small towns are a drag?

Bible, the (*buy*-bull)

A collection of sixty-six books that together tell the one big story of God's plan for humankind. The Bible is the most important book in the world because it's the only book that tells us the truth about God. For one thing, it tells us who God is and what he is like. It's also an instruction manual that shows us the difference between right and wrong. But most importantly, the Bible tells us how much God loves us and explains how we can have a relationship with him through his Son Jesus. Definitely a must read!

birthright. See *oldest son*. (*berth*-rite)

blasphemy (*blas*-fem-ee)

Speaking evil things about God. This includes misusing God's name by saying false things about him or using God's name as a curse word. Blasphemy is a terrible sin because it denies how great God is and how much he loves us.

bless

To wish God's goodness upon someone. This is often done through prayer, saying kind words to others, and treating them with kindness. (And saying, "Bless you!" when they sneeze!) God blesses us by giving us life, family, friends, and possessions. His greatest blessing is forgiving our sins and giving us eternal life.

Blessings, the (*bless*-ings)

The sermon Jesus gave in Matthew 5, also called the Beatitudes. The word *beatitude* means "blessed" or "happy." This sermon describes the attitudes God wants us to have. Jesus says we'll be blessed when we are spiritually needy, merciful, and honest or when we're rejected for being his disciples.

blind/blindness

Being unable to see. Blindness can be caused by a birth defect, damage to the eyes, or old age. Jesus healed many people who were blind. The Bible also says people can be spiritually blind, which means they can't see the truth (2 Corinthians 4:3–4).

blood (blud)

That red juice in our bodies that keeps us alive. In the Bible, blood represents life. Sin causes death, so that's why blood had to be shed in animal sacrifices to temporarily pay the price for sin. We no longer sacrifice animals to deal with sin. Jesus' blood shed on the cross dealt with sin once and for all!

Boaz (*bow*-az)

A rich man from the tribe of Benjamin who married Ruth after her husband died. Their son named Obed was King David's grandfather and Jesus' great-great granddad.

body (*bo*-dee)

The physical part of who we are. The Bible says a believer's body is the temple of the Holy Spirit (1 Corinthians 6:19). The church is also compared with a body. Just as we need every finger and eyeball for our body to work properly, we need every person in the church for *it* to work properly.

born again

To be "born of God's Spirit." Everyone is born once physically. But when Adam and Eve sinned, they were separated from God and their spirits died. Now everyone is born sinful and separated from God. But thanks to Jesus, when we put our faith in him, our spirits are reborn!

bread (bred)

Believe it or not, bread plays an important role throughout the Bible. In the Old Testament, it was used in festivals and sacrifices to God. It was important, sure, but Jesus warned that we don't "live only on bread" (Matthew 4:3–4). He also told us to "break bread" (take Communion) in memory of him. Jesus even referred to himself as bread from heaven (John 6:35).

bribe (brīb)

A form of cheating where someone is secretly paid to do something illegal or dishonest. In Bible times, some people bribed judges to decide in their favor (Amos 5:12). Judas received a bribe to betray Jesus. The Bible says giving or accepting a bribe is wrong. In the long run, cheaters cheat only themselves.

bride (brīd)

A woman who is about to be or has recently been married. The Bible compares God's relationship with Israel with that of a bridegroom and his bride. In the New Testament, the church is also called the bride of Christ (Revelation 19:7). What a wedding that's going to be!

brother (*bru*-ther)

A male sibling. The Bible talks of many famous brothers, including Cain and Abel, Moses and Aaron, Jacob and Esau, and in the New Testament, James and John (also known as the Sons of Thunder). Christians are also called Christ's brothers (Romans 8:29) and are told to love each other like brothers (brothers who get along, that is).

bully (*bull*-lee)

Someone who uses size and strength to take advantage of other people and push them around. Famous Bible bullies include Cain, Pharaoh, Goliath, Samson, and Nebuchadnezzar. If a bully pushes you around, don't put up with it, but don't fight back. Just tell your parents or a teacher.

burnt offering (bernt *off*-er-ing)

In Old Testament times, priests burned the flesh of a lamb each morning and night to pay for people's sins. Only ashes were left. We don't do this anymore because Jesus, the Lamb of God, was sacrificed for our sin once and for all. Good news for you and lambs everywhere!

C

Caesar (*see*-zer)

The title given to the ruler (emperor) of the Roman Empire. When Jesus was born, Augustus was Caesar. After Augustus was Tiberius. Next came Claudius and then Nero, a seriously nasty guy who began a terrible persecution of Christians. Domitian was the Caesar who exiled John to the island of Patmos.

Caesarea (see-zer-*ree*-ah)
An important seaport and the Roman capital of Israel. It was built by Herod the Great and named after Caesar. Peter went there to witness to Cornelius, and Philip reared four daughters there. The apostle Paul was imprisoned in Caesarea for two years before going to Rome.

Caiaphas (*kie*-a-fas)
The high priest who insisted that Pilate crucify Jesus. Caiaphas and the other members of the Sanhedrin loved their power and authority. They were afraid Jesus would mess things up, so they made up false charges and arrested him. Later Caiaphas persecuted Peter, John, and other Christians. A real swell guy.

Cain (kane)
Adam and Eve's firstborn son. When Cain, a farmer, offered some of his crops to the Lord, God rejected his offering because a blood sacrifice was required. However, God accepted his brother Abel's offering, because Abel gave an animal sacrifice as God had instructed. Cain was so jealous that he killed Abel. He then went out and built the world's first city.

Caleb (*kay*-leb)
One of the twelve spies Moses sent in to check out Canaan. The other spies returned scared out of their wits because of the giants they'd seen there. However, Caleb and Joshua weren't afraid because they trusted God. God allowed Caleb to live forty-five more years and capture the city of Hebron in his old age.

Calvary. See *Golgotha*. (*cal*-ver-ee)

camel (*ca*-mul)
A large, smelly, foul-tempered, desert-dwelling mammal that stores fat in a hump on its back. For thousands of years camels have been used to travel across the desert. Camels can go days without water and travel up to forty miles a day with a four-hundred-pound load on their backs.

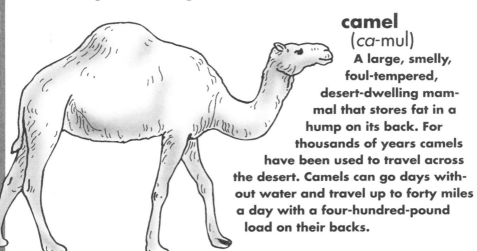

Cana (*kay*-na)

The village in Galilee where Jesus performed his first miracle: turning water into wine (John 2:1, 11). Cana was also the hometown of Nathaniel, one of Jesus' twelve apostles.

Canaan (*kay*-nan)

1. The fourth son of Ham, Noah's middle son, who was the ancestor of the Canaanites, an ungodly people who lived in the Promised Land before the Israelites went in and got rid of them. 2. The land of Canaan lay between the Jordan River and the Mediterranean Sea.

Capernaum (ka-*per*-nay-um)

A city on the Sea of Galilee. After being rejected by his hometown of Nazareth, Jesus made Capernaum his new base. This was also where he met Simon Peter, Andrew, James, and John. Strangely, the people of Capernaum rejected Jesus too (Matthew 11:23–24). Must have been something in the water.

casting lots (*cast*-ing lots)

Casting lots was used to make all kinds of decisions, from which goat to sacrifice to who should be thrown overboard (Jonah 1:7). The soldiers who crucified Jesus cast lots to decide who got his robe. It was sort of like drawing straws. These days Christians depend on God to lead them with his Spirit.

centurion (sen-*tur*-ee-on)

A Roman officer who was in charge of one hundred men or one *century*. The first centurion mentioned in the Bible asked Jesus to heal his dying servant (Matthew 8:5–10). The centurion guarding the cross confessed that Jesus was the Son of God. Cornelius was also a centurion (Acts 10:1).

chaff (chaf)

Fine, dry husks and useless broken straw produced when grain is harvested. The chaff that didn't blow away in the wind was often gathered and burned. In the Bible, chaff is used to describe worthless, evil people who are about to be destroyed (see Psalm 1:4; Matthew 3:12).

chariot (*chair*-ee-ot)

A horse-drawn vehicle used to carry soldiers quickly into battle. Chariots could be two-wheeled or four-wheeled and could carry up to four warriors. Usually one guy did the driving while the other guys shot arrows, threw spears, held up a shield to protect the others, or just tried to hold on!

cherubim (*chair*-uh-bim)

Amazing spiritual beings with many sets of wings and more than one face. A cherub (the name for a single cherubim) guarded the Garden of Eden after

Adam and Eve were sent out. Ezekiel and John saw cherubim in their visions (Ezekiel 10:14; Revelation 4:6–8).

chief priest. See *high priest.*

children (*chil*-dren)
Young people like you! Children did important things for God in the Bible. Samuel and Daniel were called to be prophets when they were boys. Josiah became king when he was eight years old. And Joash? He was crowned when he was seven. David also began serving God as a boy.

Christ (krīst)
A name for Jesus that means "Anointed One" in Greek. The Hebrew word "Messiah" also means Anointed One. The Jews had been waiting centuries for the Messiah to restore peace and rule Israel, and Jesus *was* that Messiah! (See *Jesus* and *Messiah.*)

Christmas. See *Jesus' birth.* (*kris*-mus)

Christian (*kris*-chun)
A follower of Jesus. Christians believe in God and accept that Jesus, God's Son, died as a sacrifice for their sin and rose again from the dead. Christians love and obey God. They show this love for God by loving others. Jesus' followers were first called Christians in Antioch (Acts 11:26).

church (cherch)
1. Everyone in the world who follows, has followed, and will follow Jesus. The church is also called the bride of Christ (Revelation 19:7). 2. A local group of believers, such as the church you attend. The church's job is to worship God, encourage one another, and tell others about Jesus.

circumcision (*sir*-kum-siz-zhun)
A ceremony that involved cutting off a boy's foreskin (loose skin at the tip of his penis). This was a physical sign of God's covenant with the Israelites. Circumcision was usually done eight days after birth, but Abraham had to do it as a grown man. Can you say *"ouch"*?

Claudius (*klow*-dee-us)
The fourth emperor of the Roman Empire (10 B.C.–A.D. 54). He first favored Jews and then gave them the boot out of Rome. Pretty wishy-washy, huh? The apostle Paul's friends Aquila and Priscilla were forced to leave Rome because of Claudius's law.

clean (kleen)

Pure or holy. In the Old Testament, God divided animals, things, and (under certain circumstances) even people into "clean" and "unclean" categories. Only those that were clean could be used in worship. We are all unclean because of sin, but we can become clean again by accepting Jesus as our Savior.

cloak (klōk)

A thick, woolen, outer garment worn in Bible times. It had a hole for the head and slits rather than sleeves for the arms. Jacob gave Joseph a fancy cloak to show that Joseph was his favorite son (Genesis 37:3). Cloaks were probably very itchy, not to mention hot.

commander (cuh-*man*-der)

A Roman officer over one thousand men (a regiment). The Roman commander of Jerusalem rescued Paul from an angry mob (see Acts 21:31–32).

commandment (cuh-*mand*-ment)

A law or rule given by God. Famous commandments include the Ten Commandments (Exodus 20) and the two greatest commandments to love God and others (Matthew 22:35–40). Commandments are different from requests in that we have to obey them, no options, no negotiations, no cutting special deals — just obey.

concubine (*konk*-u-bine)

A female slave with whom a man could have children. In Old Testament times, if a couple couldn't have children, the husband often fathered them through a concubine. That's how Ishmael was born (Genesis 16:2–3). Solomon had three hundred concubines in addition to seven hundred wives. Now *that* was downright ridiculous.

condemn/condemnation
(cun-dem/con-dem-*nay*-shun)

To declare someone guilty of a crime or sin and worthy of punishment. Although Jesus was innocent, he was condemned to death by Pilate. We are all condemned to death because of sin (Romans 6:23), but Jesus paid the penalty for our sin by dying on the cross.

confess (cun-*fess*)

To admit you have done something wrong. When you do something wrong, it is important to confess your sin to God and to whomever you have sinned against. If you don't, you'll wind up hurting your relationship with God and that person. It's a lose/lose situation.

consecrate (*con*-se-crate)

To set someone or something apart for God. In the Old Testament, the priests and objects for the temple were consecrated or set apart for God. In the New Testament, Jesus was consecrated for God. So are all believers (1 Peter 2:9).

conscience (*con*-shints)

A built-in warning system—like a fire alarm—to alert you when you're about to do wrong. Everyone has a conscience. It's God's way of helping people tell the difference between right and wrong. When you have the Holy Spirit, he makes your conscience even more sensitive.

content/contentment (cun-*tent*/cun-*tent*-ment)

To be happy with what God has given you. Jesus said, "Life is not made up of how much a person has" (Luke 12:15). True life is having a relationship with God. If you have that, you can always be happy, whether you get that remote-control car for Christmas or not!

convict/conviction (cun-*vict*/cun-*vict*-shun)

To find someone guilty. In the Bible, this word is used to describe how someone is found guilty for a crime. But it's also used to describe how our conscience condemns us for our sins. This feeling is what leads us to confess our sins and ask for forgiveness.

Corinth (*kor*-inth)

The most important port city in ancient Greece. Corinth was an immoral place, full of gambling, prostitution, and other sinful practices. The apostle Paul helped establish a large church there on his second missionary journey and wrote 1 and 2 Corinthians to the Christians of Corinth.

Cornelius (kor-*neel*-ee-us)

A Roman centurion who wanted to find salvation. God told Cornelius to send for Peter and then told Peter that Cornelius's men were coming. Peter went with them and preached the gospel to Cornelius and his household. They all became Christians, the first non-Jews to become believers (Acts 10).

cornerstone (*kor*-ner-stone)
A large, perfectly straight stone placed at the corner of two walls to align them and hold them together. The cornerstone was the most important stone of all. If it were straight, the whole building would be in line. The Bible says Jesus is the cornerstone of the church (Ephesians 2:20–21). He keeps us in line.

Council. See *Sanhedrin.* (*cown*-sill)

counselor (*cown*-sill-er)
Someone older and wiser than you who gives you advice (counsel) or helps you make decisions. The Holy Spirit is also our Counselor (John 14:26). He gives us wisdom and reminds us of God's Word. Need help? Don't be afraid to ask!

covenant (*cov*-eh-nent)
A serious agreement between two persons or groups. God made several covenants with people. He promised Abraham that every nation would be blessed through him. Later God made a covenant with Israel and gave them the Law. When the people couldn't keep the Law, God gave them a new covenant: Everyone who believed in Jesus would be forgiven for their sins. This covenant is for you too!

covet (*cov*-et)
To long for something that belongs to someone else; for example, really wanting a computer game your friend has. Coveting is wrong, because people who covet are never satisfied. No matter how much they have, they still want more. So don't let your eyes wander. Just be content with what you have.

creation (kree-*ay*-shun)
Everything that exists. In the beginning, there was nothing: no sound, no light, no people—not even time or space—only God. Then God spoke, and everything came into being, exactly as he created it—stars, planets, plants, animals, you name it! Wouldn't it be nice to be able to do your housework that way?

Crete (kreet)
A large island off the coast of Greece. The ship carrying the apostle Paul to his trial in Rome ran into a terrible storm off the south coast of Crete. The sailors

were scared out of their wits (Acts 27:7–21). Paul's helper Titus was overseer of the churches in Crete.

crown of life (krown)
The reward we will receive in heaven if we are faithful to God. This crown is not like a king's crown. It is more like the olive wreath that was given to athletes in the ancient Olympics (Revelation 2:10). The best part is, it'll look great with whatever you wear!

crown of thorns (krown)
A crown made of thorny branches twisted together. The Roman soldiers jammed it onto Jesus' head to make fun of him after he claimed to be the king of the Jews (Matthew 27:27–29). The joke was on them, however. Jesus really *was* king—in fact, the King of Kings!

cross (kross)
A tall, wooden post crossed by a shorter beam near the top. Today people wear gold crosses, but the Romans used crosses to make criminals suffer horribly before they died. The reason that Christians love the symbol of the cross is because Jesus died on one to give us eternal life.

crucifixion (crew-si-*fix*-shun)
People were nailed to a cross through their hands and feet, then left to die. It was a slow, very painful death. People who were crucified usually died of suffocation, because it was difficult to breathe while hanging in such an awkward position.

cud (kud)
Food that is chewed twice. Because grass is difficult to digest, animals that feed on it, such as cows, must burp it back up for a second chew. Mmmm . . . yummy! God told the Israelites they could eat any animal that chews its cud and had hoofs that were separated.

curse (kerse)
In Bible times cursing didn't mean swearing. A curse was a prayer for something terrible to happen to someone. It was no joke either. People really believed curses could come true—and they often did! Jesus told us to bless others, not curse them.

Curse, the (kerse)
The penalty for Adam and Eve's disobedience. The Curse causes everyone and everything in the world to be affected by sin and death. That's the bad news. The good news is that you can escape the Curse if you believe in Jesus!

Cyprus (*sigh*-pruss)
A large island off the coast of modern-day Turkey. Cyprus was famous for its copper mines and cypress trees. It was called Chittim in the Old Testament. Barnabas came from Cyprus, Christians fled there after the persecution in Jerusalem, and the apostle Paul started his first missionary journey there.

Cyrus the Great (*sigh*-russ)
The powerful ruler of the Persian Empire who freed the Israelites from captivity in Babylon and allowed them to go home and rebuild their temple. Cyrus was a wise and generous ruler whom God called his "shepherd" (Isaiah 44:28). Not bad for a guy who wasn't even a Jew!

Dagon (*day*-gone)
The chief Philistine fish god. Samson got his iron fingers on the stone pillars and tore down one of Dagon's temples. Another time, a statue of Dagon did a face plant and smashed in front of the Ark of the Covenant (1 Samuel 5:1–7).

Damascus (dah-*mas*-cus)
The capital of ancient Aram (Syria) and the oldest continually occupied city in the world. At times Israel fought against Damascus. The apostle Paul was on his way to arrest Christians in Damascus when he met Jesus. He later escaped from the city by (get *this!*) going over the wall in a basket.

Dan
Jacob's fifth son and father of one of the twelve tribes of Israel. The tribe of Dan received the tiniest chunk of land in Israel — and even worse, it was right on the Philistine border! However, their land was very fertile. Samson was the most famous Danite.

dance (dants)
Movement of the body in time with music. In Bible times, dancing was how Jews celebrated victories in battle, holidays, and weddings. Today some Christians still dance for the Lord as part of their worship. Other Christians prefer to just clap or sing.

Daniel (*dan*-yul)

A prophet best known for spending a night in a den of starving lions without getting a scratch (Daniel 6:7–24). God blessed Daniel in many ways, helping him learn the wisdom of the Babylonians, giving him the ability to interpret dreams, and making him a respected ruler.

Darius (da-*rye*-us)

The name of several kings in ancient Persia. The best known was Darius the Mede, who gave Daniel an important role in his government. Darius was later tricked into throwing Daniel to the lions for praying to God (Daniel 6:7–24). Darius eventually came to believe in God.

David (*day*-vid)

The greatest king of Israel and an ancestor of Jesus. David was a remarkable guy — so remarkable that God called him "a man after my own heart" and promised his kingdom would last forever. This promise was fulfilled through Jesus, who was born to Mary and Joseph, David's descendants.

deacon (*dee*-kin)

A servant or minister in a church. Deacons started out waiting on tables and making sure everyone had enough to eat. Later some of them became spiritual leaders and evangelists. We still have deacons today. They are Christians who help the pastor or minister.

Dead Sea, the (ded-see)

A salty, inland sea, the lowest body of water on earth. It is called the *Dead* Sea because water flows in but doesn't flow out, making it become stagnant or "dead." The water's so full of minerals and salt, you can float without trying.

death (deth)

The end of life. After Adam and Eve sinned, all living things began dying. Everything eventually dies, including plants, animals, and people. But remember — life on earth is not all there is. After we die, we can live forever with God.

Deborah (*deb*-orah)

A judge and prophetess of Israel. Deborah usually sat under a palm tree — not a coconut palm, fortunately — judging cases. God had Deborah tell Barak to fight the Canaanites, but Barak wouldn't do it without her. Deborah agreed to help, went along, and gave the orders to charge. *Some* lady!

debt (det)

When you borrow money and can't immediately repay it. When times were tough in Bible days, poor people borrowed money and repaid it when things improved. However, sometimes things didn't improve, and they got in over their heads. If this happened, they sometimes sold themselves into slavery to pay off the debt.

dedicate (*ded*-i-kate)

To set something or someone apart for service to God. This is usually done through some sort of religious ceremony. Many things were dedicated to God, including articles used in the temple, homes, and even babies. We still dedicate these sorts of things to God — including babies!

Delilah (duh-*lie*-la)

Samson's wife, a Philistine, who cried and whined until he told her his secret — that he'd lose his great strength if he had a haircut. Once Samson told Delilah, she called in the troops while he was sleeping. They chopped his long hair off and took him away, minus his super power.

Demas (*dee*-mas)

A companion of the apostle Paul who was in prison with him at Rome (the first time Paul was thrown into the slammer there). Later Demas deserted Paul. Seems he could never completely give up his old life for God (2 Timothy 4:10).

Demetrius (duh-*mee*-tree-us)

A silversmith who made small statues of Diana (also called Artemis), the chief goddess of Ephesus. He was so upset that the gospel would cut in on his business that he started a riot against Paul. The city clerk saved the day, but Paul hit the road anyway (Acts 19:23–41). He knew when he wasn't wanted.

demons (*dee*-munz)

Evil spirits. Demons are led by Satan, God's enemy. But don't be confused. Satan and his demons are nowhere *near* as powerful as God. They're more like bratty kids who need to be taught a lesson. And it's coming!

desert (*dez*-ert)
A dry, sandy region where few people, plants, or animals live. Many desert areas are mentioned in the Bible, including Edom, the Red Sea area, Judah, Beersheba, and Sinai. Jesus also went alone into the desert, where the devil tempted him (Matthew 4:1–11).

devil, the (*dev*-ul)
Liar or accuser, usually referred to as Satan. He is the leader of the angels who rebelled against God. He now spends his time trying to mess up God's plans by tempting people to sin. The devil is strong, but he's no match for Jesus. He's no match for you either if you know Jesus!

disciple (dis-*sigh*-pull)
A student or learner. Young Jews in Jesus' time who wanted to study the Bible chose a rabbi or teacher and spent time learning from him and trying to live like him. These young men — like the men who followed Jesus — were called disciples. If you follow Jesus, you're his disciple too!

discipline. See *training*. (*dis*-si-plin)

divorce (*duh*-vorse)
The permanent break-up of a marriage. God's plan is for husbands and wives to stay together until death. But sometimes couples have so many problems that they think they'd be better off apart than together. Some couples separate for a short while. Others end their relationships. That's called divorce.

doubt (*dowt*)
Lack of faith. Doubt can be a good thing sometimes. For example, if you doubt a liar, you'll avoid being tricked. But doubts can also keep you from God. Having doubts and questions isn't wrong, but wallowing in them is. Instead, ask God to help you overcome your doubts.

doctrine (*dok*-trin)
A group of beliefs about God, Jesus, humanity, and the church. Doctrines are important truths central to the Christian faith, such as, "There is one God, and Jesus is his Son." The main doctrine of Christians is summed up in the Apostles' Creed.

donkey (*don*-kee)
A beast of burden similar to a horse. Donkeys were important animals in Bible times. They carried people and goods across the country and turned millstones to grind grain. One donkey in the Bible spoke (Numbers 22:21–33). Jesus also rode a donkey into Jerusalem — not a talking one, though.

Dorcas (*door*-cus)

The Greek name for a Christian woman from Joppa whom the apostle Peter raised from the dead (Acts 9:36–43). The name Dorcas sounds funny, but it means "Gazelle." Her Jewish name was Tabitha. Let's hope she stuck with that.

dove (duv)

A type of pigeon. Doves are gentle, timid birds that were often used for sacrifices during Old Testament times—which might be *why* they were timid. The Holy Spirit came down in the form of a dove onto Jesus during his baptism (Matthew 3:16).

dragon (*dra*-gun)

Fire-breathing, dinosaur-like flying reptile. Bad news, kids: This type of dragon never existed, not even in Bible times. In the Bible, the word *dragon* probably refers to some sort of large snake, sea monster, or humongous lizard. The Bible also uses dragons to symbolize evil things, like Satan (see Revelation 12:3–4).

dream (dreem)

Images that pass through your mind while you're sleeping. God sometimes speaks to people through dreams. Joseph had a dream that caused his brothers to sell him into slavery. Later he interpreted Pharaoh's dream and was freed from prison. God also told another Joseph, Jesus' earthly father, that Mary's baby was from God—in a dream.

drunk/drunkenness (*drunk*-en-ness)

The condition someone is in after drinking too much alcohol. People who are drunk have trouble making decisions and controlling their bodies—especially their tongues! People thought the disciples were drunk on the Day of Pentecost (Acts 2:1–15). Not a chance!

eagle (*e*-gull)

A large, majestic bird that gently cares for its young and uses its keen eyesight to find prey before swooping down to kill it. Eagles are used as signs of God's care (Deuteronomy 32:11–12) and his judgment (Jeremiah 48:40).

E

earthquake (erth-kwake)

Shaking of the earth caused by disturbances beneath the earth's crust. Earthquakes are used throughout the Bible as symbols of God's power. An earthquake shook Jerusalem when Jesus was crucified (Matthew 27:51–54). Another earthquake happened when he was resurrected (Matthew 28:2). "A whole lotta shakin'" was going on.

Ecclesiastes (eh-*kleez*-ee-*as*-teez)

A book of wisdom from the Old Testament that tries to answer the question, What is the meaning of life? This book was written by Solomon once he had reached the top and realized that fame and riches weren't all that they were cracked up to be.

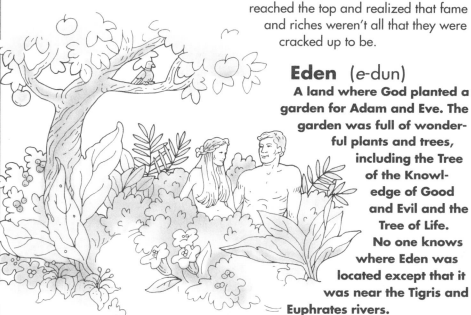

Eden (e-dun)

A land where God planted a garden for Adam and Eve. The garden was full of wonderful plants and trees, including the Tree of the Knowledge of Good and Evil and the Tree of Life. No one knows where Eden was located except that it was near the Tigris and Euphrates rivers.

Edom (e-dom)

1. The name given to Esau after he sold his inheritance (birthright) to his brother Jacob for a pot of red bean stew. (He must have really been hungry!)
2. The dry, hilly land south of the Dead Sea, occupied by Esau's descendants, the Edomites.

Egypt (e-gipt)

A country in northeast Africa located on the Nile River. Many Bible events happened in Egypt. Joseph was sold into slavery there and ended up as the ruler of Egypt. The Israelites were slaves in Egypt for 430 years until Moses led them out. Joseph, Jesus' father, fled to Egypt with Mary to escape Herod.

Ehud (e-hud)

The southpaw judge who plunged a homemade knife deep into the guts of Eglon, king of Moab. Eglon was so fat that the knife disappeared—handle and all! Then Ehud made a run for it, gathered his friends together, and laid a licking on the Moabites like they had never seen.

elder (el-der)

A leader of a church, tribe, town, or nation. Like the name implies, elders were usually older members of a group who used their wisdom and experience to guide their people. We still have elders in the church. They help the pastor and guide believers in the faith.

Eli (e-lie)

The judge and high priest who raised Samuel. After God answered Hannah's prayer for a son, she brought her son, Samuel, to be raised at the temple by Eli. Eli was a good priest but a poor father, and he and his sons were punished for their sins.

Elijah (e-lie-jah)

The prophet who called down fire from heaven. He was also known as the running prophet. First he ran from Ahab after prophesying against him. Then he outran a chariot. Then he ran from Ahab's wife Jezebel after slaughtering Baal's prophets. No wonder he went up to heaven in a whirlwind (2 Kings 2:1–11). He never slowed down!

Elisha (e-lie-sha)

The main prophet to Israel after Elijah. Through the Holy Spirit, Elisha prophesied, advised, and anointed kings. He also helped the needy and performed many miracles, such as raising a boy from the dead and striking a whole army blind. Unfortunately for him, he was also quite bald!

Elizabeth (e-liz-uh-beth)

Mother of John the Baptist and wife of Zechariah the priest. She was also Mary's cousin. Elizabeth and Zechariah couldn't have children, but God performed a miracle and she became pregnant. "Jumpin' John" leaped in Elizabeth's womb when Mary came to visit while pregnant with Jesus!

end times, the

The period of time between the first and second coming of Jesus when the conflict between God and Satan reaches its final stage. This period will end with a great tribulation, during which God judges the earth. Many terrible things will happen, but it will all work out in the end.

enjoyment. See *entertainment.* (en-*joy*-munt)

Enoch (*e*-knock)
1. Cain's eldest son. The first city mentioned in the Bible was named after Enoch. 2. The father of Methuselah. Enoch was taken up into heaven and never had to die. Wouldn't that be cool? He also got to live for three hundred years!

entertainment (en-ter-*tane*-munt)
Enjoyment or amusement (Daniel 6:18). In Bible times, people had only live entertainment. Just imagine — no TV, no video games, and no Internet! But they did have board games, sports, singing, dancing, and drama. We should always make sure our entertainment choices line up with God's word (Philippians 4:8).

Epaphroditus (e-*paf*-fro-*die*-tus)
A messenger from the church in Phillipi who delivered a gift to the apostle Paul while Paul was under house arrest in Rome. Epaphroditus became sick while in Rome, but when he recovered, Paul sent him home with a letter that became the book of Philippians in the Bible.

Ephesus (*eh*-fe-sus)
A large trade city on the west coast of what is now Turkey. It was known for its huge temple to the goddess Artemis (also called Diana). The apostle Paul lived in Ephesus for three years and started a large church there. The book of Ephesians was a letter Paul wrote to Christians in Ephesus.

Ephraim (e-fray-um)
The second son of Joseph and founder of one of the twelve tribes of Israel. Jacob gave Ephraim the blessing that normally would have gone to Ephraim's older brother, Manasseh. What can you say? God knew he was an exceptional kid.

Esau (e-saw)
Isaac's elder son. Esau was a rough, tough, hairy-chested, outdoorsy type of guy who loved to hunt — unlike his brother Jacob who hung around the kitchen. As the elder son, Esau was supposed to receive the birthright from his father. But he sold it to Jacob for a pot of stew. Not exactly the swiftest move.

Esther (es-ter)
A beautiful Jewish girl who won a royal beauty contest and was chosen by the king of Persia to be his new queen. God used Esther's influence to save her cousin Mordecai and the Jews from being killed by the evil Haman. Read all about it in the book of Esther.

eternity/eternal (e-*ter*-ni-tee/e-*ter*-null)

A period of time without beginning or end. Can you imagine something that big and long? Kind of makes your head spin, doesn't it? Only God is eternal, but he promises to give us everlasting life if we believe in Jesus (Romans 6:23).

Ethiopia/Ethiopian
(e-thee-*o*-pee-uh/e-thee-*o*-pee-un)

An ancient African country south of Egypt. The northern parts of Ethiopia were called Nubia and Cush. Noah's son Ham was the father of Cush and was likely the ancestor of the Ethiopians. The most famous Ethiopian in the Bible is the eunuch whom Philip witnessed to (Acts 8:26–40).

Euphrates River (you-*fray*-tees)

A major river that flowed through ancient Syria, Assyria, Mesopotamia, and the city of Babylon. Many people lived along the Euphrates (including Abraham when he was in Ur), because it was the main source of water in that dry region. It was also the northern border of the Promised Land.

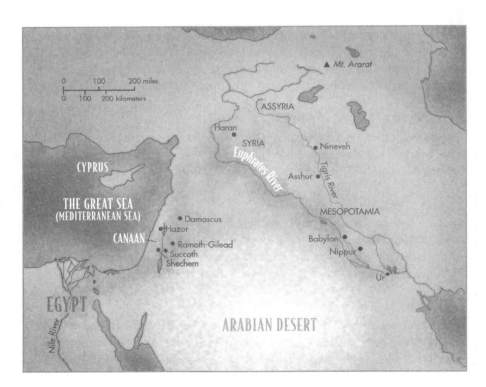

evangelist (e-*van*-gel-ist)
Someone who tells others the good news about Jesus. This word is also used to describe the writers of the four Gospels — Matthew, Mark, Luke, and John. As Christians, we are all called to be evangelists, sharing the love of God with people we know (Matthew 28:18–19).

evil (e-*vul*)
Bad or sinful. Anything that goes against God or displeases him is evil. This includes selfish attitudes, treating others poorly, and ignoring God. Ever since Adam and Eve sinned, humans have wanted to do evil. Satan also tempts us to do bad things. But we can overcome evil through Jesus.

evil spirit. See *demons*. (e-*vul speer*-it)

Exile, the. See *prisoners in Babylon*. (x-ile)

Exodus, the (ex-uh-dus)
"Going out." The second book in the Bible is called Exodus because it tells the story of how God used Moses (and miracles) to deliver millions of Israelites from Egypt. Exodus describes them going out from Egypt, where they had been slaves for 430 years.

exorcism (ex-or-sism)
When spiritual leaders order a demon or an evil spirit to leave someone's body. Jesus performed many exorcisms while on earth (e.g., Mark 1:23–26; 5:2–13), as did his disciples (Matthew 10:1). Some priests and pastors still do exorcisms today on rare occasions.

Ezekiel (eh-*zee*-kee-ul)
A prophet to the Jews while they were prisoners in Babylon. Ezekiel had many strange and amazing visions, wilder than any computer special effects. For example, his vision of "wheels within wheels" almost makes you dizzy (Ezekiel 1). He also saw skeletons come back to life. Creepy but cool.

Ezra (*ez*-ra)
A Jewish priest from Persia. After the Exile — and some sixty years after the temple was rebuilt — God and the king of Persia sent Ezra back to Jerusalem to get the Jews to clean up their act. Ezra did a good job, and the Jews began obeying God's law once again.

F

faith

Believing in something you *can't* see based on something you can see. Faith is a powerful thing. The tiniest amount can move mountains (Matthew 17:20). But faith isn't like magic. Faith is built on God's promises in the Bible. Faith reads the promises and believes that the God who made the promises will keep them.

faithful (*faith*-full)

Solid, dependable, trustworthy, and reliable. The Bible tells us God is faithful (Hebrews 10:23). That means we can count on him to come through on his promises. God also wants *us* to be faithful. In other words, if you promise to clean up your room, make sure you do it!

family (*fam*-i-lee)

Your parents, brothers, sisters, aunts, uncles — every relative you have. God created families to help you grow up and make sure there's always someone who cares for you. When you become a Christian, you join the family of God, which includes every Christian on earth!

family wealth (*fam*-i-lee welth)

Money, land, and other property passed from one generation to the next. It is also called an inheritance. It's good for parents to pass on material wealth to their children, but the best inheritance of all is godly character. You can inherit this by obeying your parents and following their example.

famine (*fam*-in)

When there's not enough food to eat. Famine was a constant threat during Bible times, because the rain had to fall at just the right time or the crops would fail. One famine in Egypt lasted seven years. Famines also happened inside a city when enemy armies surrounded them.

fast(ing) (*fast*-ing)

Going without food and sometimes water, usually to show dedication to God. People also fasted when they were mourning a death or disaster. Christians still fast today to draw closer to God. When you *fast*, time goes really *slow*.

father (*fa*-ther)

A male parent. Jesus often referred to God as his "Father in heaven." He told his disciples God is *our* Father in heaven as well (Matthew 7:11). This means we can have a loving, close relationship with God just like we're supposed to have with our father on earth! Cool, isn't it?

feast (feest)

A huge meal held to celebrate a special occasion. When God made his covenant with the Israelites, he ordered them to celebrate several different feasts. (Now *this* had to be an easy commandment to keep!) These feasts marked important events in Israel's history, such as harvests and their escape from Egypt.

Feast of Booths

This celebration helped the Jews remember their wanderings in the wilderness. It was also called the Feast of Tabernacles. During this feast, they built temporary shelters (booths) out of palm branches and willow trees to remind them of the temporary shelters the Israelites had in the desert.

Feast of Hanukkah (*Ha*-nu-kah)

This feast celebrated the cleansing of the temple after it had been made unclean by Antiochus Epiphanes. It was also known as the Feast of Dedication or the Festival of Lights. Jewish people still celebrate this feast today just before Christmas.

Feast of Weeks

This festival took place at the beginning of the harvest season. It was also called the Feast of Harvest. The Jews celebrated this feast to thank God for the crops to come. By New Testament times, it became known as Pentecost. The believers received the Holy Spirit on this day.

Feast of Passover. See *Passover.* (*pass*-o-ver)

Feast of Unleavened Bread (un-*leh*-vind)
A festival that celebrated God setting the Israelites free from Egypt. It began the day after the Feast of Passover. During this feast, the Jews ate bread made without yeast just like they did when they left Egypt in such a big hurry.

Felix (*fee*-licks)
A corrupt Roman governor of Judea. The apostle Paul appeared before him after being accused of disturbing the peace. Felix liked Paul and hoped he would offer him a bribe to get out of prison. The bribe never came, so Paul sat in the slammer until Felix lost his job.

fellowship (*fell*-o-ship)
Sharing life and having things in common with others. Fellowship is a good thing, but you have to be careful whom you share life with. Fellowship with the wrong people, and they'll drag you down. Hang out with the right people, and they'll lift you up. Pretty simple, isn't it?

fig
A small, sweet fruit that grows in the Middle East. Something like giant raisins, figs were usually dried and then eaten. Jesus made a fig tree wither because it had no figs on it (Mark 11:13–14). He did this to show his disciples we all need to bear fruit for God.

Festus (*fes*-tus)
The governor of Judea after Felix. Paul's religious enemies tried to trick Festus into sending Paul from Caesarea to Jerusalem so they could kill him. When Festus gave Paul a choice, Paul chose to be judged by Caesar instead. Festus thought Paul was innocent but sent him to Rome.

fire
In the Bible, fire was often a symbol of God's presence and power. God got Moses' attention with a burning bush. He also led the Israelites through the wilderness with a pillar of fire by night. In the New Testament, tongues of fire appeared above the disciples' heads at Pentecost.

firstfruits (*ferst*-frutes)
The firstborn animals in a flock or herd or the first crops gathered at harvest time. God taught the Jewish people that these belonged to him and were to be offered to him during the Feast of Weeks as a way of thanking him.

fish

Jesus often used fish or fishing in his parables (Matthew 13:47–50). He also used fish to perform miracles (Matthew 17:24–27). During the early days of the church, the fish became a symbol for Christianity. Christians still stick fish symbols on their cars. When they do, they should watch how they drive!

flesh

1. Our physical bodies. 2. That part of us which is sinful, mean, and selfish. Another name for the flesh is the "sinful nature." We can overcome the flesh with the help of the Holy Spirit. Make sure your spirit is willing to obey God if your flesh is weak!

Flood, the (flud)

Water that covered the entire earth. God punished the sinful ancient world by sending so much rain that the whole world flooded. Noah and his family rode out the Flood in the ark, a huge ship filled with two of every type of clean animal. After forty days and nights of rain, the Flood ended, the ground dried, and Noah's family started all over again.

food

What we eat in order to live. Food is important (and yummy), but you should always eat to live rather than live to eat. Eating too much of anything — no matter how good it tastes — is called gluttony, and that's a sin. Remember that the next time you're tempted to go for a fourth helping of ice cream.

foolishness (*foo*-lish-ness)

The opposite of wisdom. There are *serious* foolish people and *foolish* foolish people. Serious foolishness is when people don't take advice and refuse to change. Foolish foolishness is when people do or say just about anything to get attention or make people laugh. Sound like anyone you know? Hopefull, not the person you see in the mirror!

forgiveness (for-*giv*-ness)

Not holding a grudge against someone who has wronged you. Through Jesus, God has forgiven us for everything we've ever done wrong. He wants us to follow this example by forgiving others just as we have been forgiven. Instead of grinding an axe, bury it. Forgive!

fornication (forn-ih-*cay*-shun)

When single people have a sexual relationship outside of marriage. Fornication is different from adultery. Adultery involves married people, while fornication does not. However, it is still a very serious sin because it goes against God's plan for sex.

friend (frend)

People who share interests and enjoy spending time together. True friends stand by each other no matter what, just like Jonathan and David did (1 Samuel 18:1). Even Jesus had a special friend (John 13:23). Jesus wants to be your friend too. You can become his friend by following him.

frog

An amphibian known for croaking, jumping, and zapping out its tongue at flies. Frogs are mentioned several times in the Bible. There was a plague of frogs in Egypt (Exodus 8:1–14), and Revelation 16:13 talks about lying demons that looked like frogs. Those would be fibbing amphibians.

fruit of the Spirit

Character qualities you have if the Holy Spirit is working in your life. These include love, joy, peace, patience, kindness, goodness, faithfulness, gentleness, and self-control (Galatians 5:22–23). It's simple — if you let God's Spirit work in you, you produce good stuff. If you don't, you produce stinky, rotten fruit.

furnace (*fer*-nuss)

An ancient stove with a fire inside, used for cooking food or melting metals. Furnaces were usually made of stone or brick and could be heated to very high temperatures. Large furnaces were used for making bricks in Babylon. This was probably the type of furnace Nebuchadnezzar tried to roast Daniel's friends in (Daniel 3:15–30).

Gabriel (gabe-ree-ull)

An angel who runs a messenger service for God. He first appeared to Daniel to explain heavenly visions. Four hundred years later, he appeared to Zechariah to tell him he would have a son. Finally, he told Mary she was going to give birth to the Savior, Jesus.

Gad

Jacob's seventh son and father of one of the twelve tribes of Israel. We don't know much about Gad's life except that he was faithful to God and probably a very strong, forceful leader (Deuteronomy 33:20–21). He also had seven sons (Numbers 26:15–18).

Gaius (*guy*-us)

1. A believer from Macedonia who went with Paul on some of his missionary journeys. 2. A believer from Derbe who traveled with Paul from Macedonia into Asia. 3. A believer from Corinth who had a church in his home. 4. A believer to whom John wrote his third letter. Wow! Popular name!

Galatia (gah-*lay*-shah)

A Roman province in Asia Minor (modern-day Turkey). Paul and Barnabas evangelized many cities in Galatia during their first missionary journey, including Pisidian Antioch, Iconium, Lystra, and Derbe. Paul returned there on his second and third journeys. The book of Galatians was written to the churches he'd founded in Galatia.

Galilee (gal-i-lee)

A well-watered, fertile area in northern Israel. It contains the Sea of Galilee, which was really a lake. Hundreds of years before Jesus was born, Isaiah prophesied that the Messiah would teach in Galilee (Isaiah 9:1–2). Sure enough, Jesus did most of his teaching there. Right on, Isaiah!

Gallio (*gall*-e-oh)

This ruler of Achaia was also a famous Roman. Some Jews in Corinth wanted Gallio to punish Paul for preaching the gospel, but Gallio told them he didn't want any part in their doctrinal squabbles and tossed the case out of court.

Gamaliel (ga-*may*-lee-el)

A member of the Sanhedrin who taught the apostle Paul. He also urged the religious leaders not to be too harsh on Christians. He figured if Jesus wasn't the Messiah, it would all blow over soon. But if he really was God's Son, no one could stop Christianity from spreading. He was right!

Garden of Eden (*gar*-dun uv *e*-dun)

The beautiful garden God created for Adam and Eve. It contained many wonderful trees and plants, not to mention amazing animals. God wanted Adam and Eve and their descendants to live there forever, but Adam and Eve disobeyed God and were forced out into the cold, cruel world.

Garden of Gethsemane (geth-*sem*-a-nee)
A grove of olive trees on the Mount of Olives that was named after the *gethsemene* there. A gethsemane was a stone basin for pressing olive oil. Jesus often went to this garden with his disciples. He was praying there the night he was betrayed and arrested.

Gaza (*ga*-zuh)
The ancient Philistine capital on the Mediterranean coast. After Samson was blinded, he had to turn a millstone to grind grain in Gaza. He later tore down the colossal temple of Dagon there. In the New Testament, Philip evangelized the Ethiopian eunuch on the road to Gaza.

Gehazi (guh-haz-ee)
The prophet Elisha's servant. He was a faithful helper until Namaan, a commander in the Syrian army, was cured of leprosy. Elisha refused to be paid, but Gehazi couldn't resist. He lied to Naaman and pocketed the reward. God showed Elisha what Gehazi had done, then Gehazi got leprosy.

Gentile (*gen*-tile)
Anyone who is not a Jew. The Jewish people knew they were special to God. They thought they were so special, in fact, they wouldn't even eat with people who weren't Jews. They thought the Messiah would come only for them. But they were wrong. Jesus came for everyone, Jews and Gentiles!

gentleness (*gen*-tull-ness)
Being kind, considerate, and loving. Gentleness is a fruit of the Spirit. When you have inner strength from God, you don't worry if kids think that being gentle means you're not tough. You can be kind to others and still be strong. God treats us with gentleness and wants us to treat others that way too.

giants (*gi*-unts)
Incredibly large human beings. And yes, they really *did* exist! The first giants mentioned in the Bible are the Nephilim (Genesis 6:4). The Israelites also ran into giants when they entered Canaan (Numbers 13:33). King Og was the last Rephaite (Deuteronomy 3:11). Goliath was also a giant.

Gideon (*gid*-ee-un)
A judge famous for testing God. When God asked Gideon to attack the Midianites, Gideon asked God for a sign to make sure he wasn't dreaming. God gave it to him. Then Gideon asked for another sign! God gave that too. Then he helped Gideon and three hundred soldiers whip thirty-two thousand Midianites.

gifts, spiritual (gifts, *speer*-i-chull)
Abilities given to us by God that perfectly match who he made us to be and what he wants us to do. They include things like helping, teaching, sharing words of wisdom — even healing! Ever wondered what your gifts are? Ask God to show you!

Gilboa (gil-*bow*-ah)
A ridge of mountains half a mile east of the city of Jezreel. A huge, terrible battle raged on Mount Gilboa between Israel and the Philistines in which Saul and his sons were killed (1 Chronicles 10).

Gilead (*gilly*-ad)
Gilead founded the tribe of the Gileadites. They settled in a mountain region east of the Jordan River, "the land of Gilead." This land was famous for the balm (healing ointment) of Gilead. And of course, there was the city of Gilead in the hilly land of Gilead where Gilead's lads lived.

giving (*giv*-ing)
Willingly handing over what you have to someone else. God is generous and asks us to be like him by giving to others. By sharing with others you show that you love God and trust him to provide for you. You *do* trust God, don't you?

glory (*glor*-ee)
The beauty, power, and honor of God. God's glory is visible in nature, in other people, and in anything beautiful. God also revealed his glory in special ways in the Bible, such as the pillar of fire that led the Israelites through the wilderness. Jesus is the clearest picture of God's glory.

goat (gote)
A horned, hairy, little grass-eater. The Israelites ate goats and used their skins as bottles for water and wine. Goats were also used in sacrifices to God. The goats that escaped from being sacrificed were called scapegoats (and lucky). Each year, a scapegoat was let loose in the desert to carry away the Israelites' sins.

God
The maker and ruler of everything. God is so great that he is beyond our understanding. But he has told us many things about himself in the Bible. For one, he created the universe. Second, he is spirit, which means he doesn't have a body. God also knows *everything,* exists *everywhere* at once, and can do *anything.* Now here's the tricky part. He also exists as three persons: Father, Son, and Holy Spirit. (Told you he is hard to understand!) This is called the Trinity. Best of all, God is love, and he wants to have a relationship with *you* through his son Jesus!

godly (*god*-lee)
To be like God, to live the kind of life God wants you to live. This means being kind, patient, loving, forgiving, and all-around doing what's right. But you can't be like this on your own no matter how hard you try. You need the power of God's Spirit working in you.

godly sadness (*god*-lee *sad*-nuss)
The terrible feeling you get when you do something wrong and determine not to do it again. This is also called repentance. When you feel godly sadness and ask God to forgive you, you can be certain he will. Jesus died so that *all* of our sins could be forgiven.

gold
A rare, beautiful, and precious metal. Gold was often used as money during Bible times. King Solomon collected twenty-five tons of gold in taxes each year. That's equal to the weight of about twenty-five cars! The Bible says the streets of heaven are also paved with gold (Revelation 21:21).

golden calf (*goal*-dun caf)

An idol of a young bull made by the Israelites while Moses was up on Mount Sinai receiving the Ten Commandments. When Moses came down, he was so angry at what they'd done, he smashed the Ten Commandments. Then he ground the calf into powder, mixed it with water, and made the Israelites *drink* it! Yuck!

Golgotha (*gol*-goth-a)

"Place of the skull." The Aramaic name for the hill outside Jerusalem where the Romans crucified criminals. This was where Jesus was crucified. The Roman name for Golgotha was Calvary—the Skull—probably because it resembled a skull.

Goliath (go-*lie*-ath)

A Philistine giant who would make any NBA player look like a shrimp. Goliath challenged the Israelites to send one man—count it, *one* man—to fight him. Not one Israelite stepped forward. Then David took the challenge. With one well-slung stone from his sling, David downed that dangerous dude. See also *bully*.

good(ness)

Always doing what's right. God is good. That means he's always righteous, holy, kind, pure, honest, fair, generous, trustworthy, merciful, and loving. That's quite a list! God wants you to have goodness too. If you obey the leading of God's Spirit in your heart, you will.

Goshen (*go*-shen)

An area in the eastern Nile delta (in Egypt) where the soil was super rich. Joseph and his family settled there while he was prime minister of Egypt (Genesis 46:28). Goshen was protected against the plagues of flies and hail when God poured his plagues on Egypt to bust the Israelites out of slavery.

gospel (gos-pull)

1. "Good news" in Greek. We were all condemned to die under the curse of sin. (That's the *bad* news!) The good news is that God sent his son Jesus to die for us, then come back to life, defeating sin and death. Now we can overcome sin and death too. All we have to do is believe in Jesus, confess our sins, and accept his forgiveness. 2. The story of Jesus' life. There are four Gospels in the Bible: Matthew, Mark, Luke, and John. Each man tells his story from a different angle.

gossip (gos-sip)

Saying things about others that are bad, untrue, or both. Gossip hurts everyone. When you gossip, you damage reputations — especially your own — because you show you can't be trusted. Then no one wants to be your friend. Next time you feel the urge to gossip, give your tongue a rest.

government (guv-er-munt)

The rulers of a country who govern (rule), make laws, provide services like school, and keep the peace. In Jesus' time, the Romans governed much of the world. Even though they weren't always kind to Christians, the apostle Paul told believers to obey the government (Romans 13:5). We should obey our government too.

grace (grayse)

A free, undeserved gift. Everyone is a sinner. Because of that, we don't deserve eternal life in heaven. But God is willing to give it to us anyway. It works like this. Jesus died on the cross and paid the penalty for our sins. Now all we have to do is believe in him, admit we have sinned, and accept God's grace.

Greece (greese)

A country in southern Europe between Italy and Turkey. Alexander the Great expanded the Greek Empire until it filled the entire Middle East. He brought Greek culture, language, and ideas to the entire ancient world. Even though the Greeks no longer ruled in Jesus' day, people in Israel still spoke and wrote in Greek.

greed

Wanting more than we need. Greed causes us to mistreat or push ahead of others to get what we want. It's also a sign that we don't trust God to provide for us. Avoiding greed is easy — just focus on giving to others rather than getting things for yourself!

guarding your heart (*gard*-ing yore hart)

Protecting your heart from bad things. Many people watch garbage on TV thinking it won't affect them. But junk entertainment is like junk food — it may taste good, but it's terrible for you! Foolish folks fill their hearts with filth. (Say that quickly five times.) Wise people fill their hearts with God's wisdom.

guilt. See *godly sadness.* (gilt)

Hagar (*hay*-gar)

Abraham's concubine and the mother of Ishmael. When Abraham and Sarah couldn't have children, Sarah told Abraham to have a child with her servant Hagar. But after Hagar had Ishmael, Sarah had a son of her own and sent Hagar and Ishmael away. They nearly died in the wilderness, but God sent an angel to help them.

Haggai (*hay*-guy)

A prophet who lived after the Jews returned from Babylon. Together with Zechariah, Haggai encouraged the Jews to finish rebuilding God's temple. Years earlier, the Jews had been excited about the project. They just needed a little boost to get going again. The book of Haggai records Haggai's prophecies.

hallelujah (hal-le-*lu*-ya)

A Hebrew word meaning "praise the Lord." Hallelujah appears at the beginning and ending of many psalms (see Psalm 106; 111–113). This is also what the large crowd of people in heaven say when Babylon is defeated (Revelation 19:1–6). We still say "hallelujah" today to praise God.

Ham

Noah's youngest son. (No, he wasn't named after Noah's favorite pork dish!) Ham was the father of the Africans and the Egyptians. The Bible often calls Egypt "the land of Ham." Some people think Ham was cursed for disrespecting his father. Not so. Ham's son Canaan, father of the Canaanites, was the one cursed.

Haman (*hay*-men)

A dastardly dude who worked for Xerxes, the king of Persia. When Mordecai wouldn't bow down to him, evil Haman plotted to have Mordecai and all of the Jews in the Persian Empire killed (see Esther 3:1–9:25). He even built a place to hang Mordecai. But Haman got hanged there instead!

Hannah (*han*-uh)

Mother of Samuel the prophet. Hannah couldn't have children, so she promised God that if he gave her a son, she would devote the child to him. God answered her prayer, and Hannah kept her promise. She took Samuel to be reared by Eli the high priest. God then blessed Hannah with more children.

Hanukkah. See *Feast of Hanukkah*. (*han*-nu-kuh)

Haran (*hair*-ran)

1. Abraham's brother and the father of Lot. 2. A city far to the north of Canaan where Abraham and his father Terah lived for many years before Abraham went to Canaan. Later Jacob returned to Haran and lived with his relatives who were still there.

harvest (*har*-vust)

To gather crops from the field when they're ripe. Israel had three important harvest times: barley harvest in spring, wheat harvest in summer, and fruit harvest in fall. There are spiritual harvests too. Jesus said leading souls to him is like harvesting. Judgment Day will be the final harvest (Revelation 14:15).

heaven (*hev*-un)

The paradise where God and his angels live and where Christians go when they die. Heaven is a place of complete happiness. There'll be no pain, sadness, sickness, or death. Best of all, we'll live with God forever! Not something to miss out on.

healing (*heel*-ing)

To restore to health. One way Jesus showed God's love was by healing people. People brought friends and relatives who were blind, deaf, paralyzed, and crippled, and Jesus healed them all. He even brought some back from the dead (John 11)! God still heals today.

heart (hart)

In the Bible, "heart" does not just mean your ticker, the physical organ that pumps blood. Your heart is the inner part of you where your thoughts and feelings originate—who you *are* deep down inside. God wants you to love and serve him with your whole heart (Mark 12:30).

Hebrew (*he*-brew)
1. Another name for a Jew—a person descended from Abraham, Isaac, and Jacob. 2. The language the Jewish people spoke. Hebrew uses a different alphabet from English and is written right to left instead of left to right. The Old Testament is written mostly in Hebrew. Many Jews still speak Hebrew today.

Hebron (*he*-brawn)
A city located between Jerusalem and Beersheba. This was where God made a covenant with Abraham, promising to turn his descendants into a mighty nation. This was also where the angel told Abraham he would have a son, Isaac. Hebron was also David's capital for years before he took over Jerusalem.

heir (*air*)
Someone who receives an inheritance (property, money, or some other gift left behind after someone dies). In Bible times, the inheritance was usually divided among the sons in a family with a double portion going to the eldest son. As Christians, we are also heirs. What do *we* get? Eternal life!

hell
A place of separation from God where people who don't know Jesus will be sent after the Great White Throne judgment (Revelation 20:11–15). There is no love, no kindness, no caring, no good stuff at all in hell—just pain, torment, fire, and suffering. Forever.

help
To say or do something when there is a need. You should help others whenever you can. Sound like a tall order? When you have God's love in your heart, he'll show you what to do! Who knows? One day *you* may need help.

Hermon, Mount (*her*-mon)
A mountain north of the Sea of Galilee. It was a sacred place to the Canaanites who lived in Canaan before the Israelites arrived. This mountain is probably where Jesus had an astonishing transfiguration and revealed his glory to Peter, James, and John (Matthew 17:2).

Herod Antipas (*hair*-rud *an*-tee-pas)
King of Israel and son of Herod the Great. He is best known for making a boast, then beheading John the Baptist to save face (Matthew 14:6–12). His other notable evil acts include having Jesus beaten and mocked during his trial. He was a lot like his dad.

Herod Agrippa 1 (*hair*-rud ah-*grip*-pa)

King of Israel and grandson of Herod the Great. Continuing the family tradition of being an evil tyrant, he arrested Christians in an effort to get chummy with the religious leaders. But he got his just deserts when God judged him and he was eaten alive by worms (Acts 12:20–23). Yuck!

Herod Agrippa 2 (*hair*-rud ah-*grip*-pa)

The great-grandson of Herod the Great and the last ruler in the Herodian line. He was one *very* strange fellow, though he wasn't as cruel as his ancestors. He even tried to set Paul free from prison. But Paul appealed to Rome, so off to Rome he went.

Herod the Great (*hair*-ud)

The wicked king who ruled Israel under the Romans. When Herod heard that the Messiah (king of the Jews) had been born in Bethlehem, he ordered all male babies there to be slaughtered (Matthew 2:16). But an angel warned Joseph (Jesus' father) to leave *quick,* and they escaped to Egypt.

Hezekiah (hez-e-*ki*-uh)

One of Judah's most godly kings and the son of Ahaz, one of Israel's most ungodly kings. (Go figure!) Hezekiah helped his people get back on track with God. He reopened the temple, demolished pagan altars, and got everyone celebrating Passover again. God also miraculously healed Hezekiah (Isaiah 38:1–8).

high places

Sites on the tops of hills usually dedicated to worshiping false gods. In the early days, the Israelites worshiped God in high places. After the temple was built, however, the high places were off limits. But King Solomon and others often forgot this rule (e.g., 1 Kings 11:7–8).

high priest (hi preest)

Someone who acted as the go-between for the Israelites and God by offering sacrifices and prayers for the people. We don't need a high priest to talk to God for us anymore, because Jesus is our high priest now (Hebrews 4:15–16), and we can pray to God in his name.

Hittites (*hit*-ites)

One of the peoples Israel was supposed to drive out of the Promised Land. They didn't do a good job, because Hittites kept popping up. Ahimelech, one of David's closest friends, was a Hittite. So was Uriah, the man David stole Bathsheba from. Solomon also married a Hittite.

holy (*ho*-lee)

Free from sin, impurity, or evil. Only God is holy. The rest of us are all mucked up and infected with sin. But if we receive Jesus, God forgives our sins and sends his Holy Spirit to live inside us. Then we need to stay close to Jesus and out of the muck!

holy bread (*ho*-lee bred)

Twelve loaves of bread placed in the holy room of God's sanctuary each Sabbath. They were also called "showbread." This served as a reminder to the Jews that God had provided for them. Each week, the priests baked new bread then ate the old loaves. Imagine: nothing but week-old bread for your entire life!

Holy Spirit (*ho*-lee *speer*-it)

The Holy Spirit is God. He is also the third person of the Trinity, which includes God the Father and God the Son (Jesus). The Holy Spirit is like God in every way. That means he's everywhere at once, he's all-powerful, and he knows everything. He also has God's character, which means he's loving, kind, trustworthy, faithful, and every other good thing you can think of! If you're a Christian, you have the Holy Spirit in your heart right now.

holy tent (*ho*-lee tent)

Also called the Tent of Meeting or tabernacle. It was the place where the Israelites worshiped God. They used this tent while they were in the desert for forty years and for hundreds of years in the land of Israel. When Solomon built the first temple, the Israelites worshiped God there instead.

honest lives (*hon*-est lives)

Lives that fit with the rules that God gave in the Ten Commandments and the teachings that Jesus gave us. This includes telling the truth, being kind to others, and obeying our parents.

honor (*on*-er)

To show respect for or give credit to someone. Our supreme honor and respect should go to God. However, in the Ten Commandments, God also told us we should honor our parents. This means doing what they say, not talking back, and treating them with kindness. Sound like a plan?

hosanna (ho-*za*-na)

A Hebrew word meaning "save us now." This is what the people shouted when Jesus rode into Jerusalem. They did this because they believed Jesus was the Messiah who would save and restore their nation.

Hosea (ho-*zay*-ah)
A prophet to Israel just before it fell to the Assyrians. God asked Hosea to marry a sexually immoral woman (named Gomer, of all things). Her unfaithfulness to Hosea was a picture of Israel's unfaithfulness to God. You can read about it in the book of Hosea.

hospitality (hos-pi-tal-i-tee)
The ability to entertain or host people well. God commanded the Israelites to show hospitality to strangers. Good thing Abraham obeyed, because he hosted angels without even knowing it (Genesis 18:1–15)! There are many examples of good hosts in the New Testament as well, including Mary, Martha, and even Zacchaeus.

humility (hu-*mill*-i-tee)
Recognizing that all we have comes from God, including our time, talent, and resources. Humility is the opposite of pride, which makes us want to take credit for everything. Jesus showed that humility doesn't mean putting ourselves down. It means lifting others up, especially God.

hymn (him)
A song of praise to God. The book of Psalms is the Jewish hymnbook. Although we just read the psalms now, they were originally chanted or sung. Too bad we lost the music. We still sing hymns today. Many of them are even based on the psalms.

hypocrite See *pretender.* (*hip*-o-crit)

hyssop (*hih*-sop)
A part of the mint family. Hyssop comes from a small shrub with yellow flowers. Bunches of hyssop were used to smear blood on the doorposts during the first Passover. Hyssop was dipped in water and given to Jesus to quench his thirst when he was on the cross.

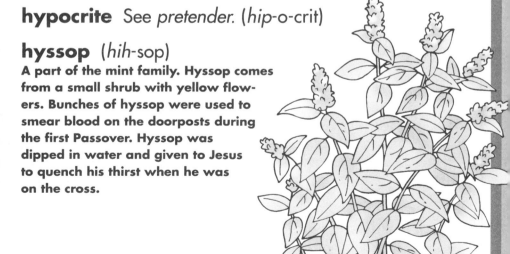

Iconium (eye-*cone*-ee-um)
The capital of Lycaonia in Asia Minor. Paul and Barnabas visited Iconium after getting booted out of Pisidian Antioch. However, things soon got hot for them in Iconium too. The people were going to stone them, so Paul and Barnabas had to run for their lives once again (Acts 14:1–6).

idol (*eye*-dull)
A statue of a false god made from clay, wood, or metal. People in Bible times worshiped idols or statues that had no power. God doesn't want us making statues of him or any other gods (Exodus 20:3–4). Loving something more than God is another form of idol worship.

image of the Beast
A statue or some other image of the Antichrist (also known as the Beast) that people will be forced to worship during the Tribulation. Anyone who doesn't worship this image will be killed (Revelation 13:14–15). Yikes!

Immanuel (i-*man*-you-el)
A name for Jesus that means "God with us" (Matthew 1:23). The name was originally used by Isaiah to describe a child who symbolized hope while Judah was under attack. Centuries later, Matthew used this title for Jesus to show how he is the ultimate hope for humankind.

incense (*in*-cents)
A mixture of four substances, including frankincense (not to be confused with Frankenstein) that gave off a sweet smell when burned. Incense was burned in the temple to show how the prayers of the Israelites were a pleasing smell to God. Some churches still burn incense during worship today.

inheritance See *family wealth*. (in-*hair*-i-tents)

integrity See *honest lives*. (in-*teh*-gri-tee)

intercession (inter-*seh*-shun)
Praying for someone else — like when Abraham prayed for the people of Sodom or Moses prayed for the Israelites. The best example of intercession is Jesus, who talks to God asking for good things for every believer (Hebrews 7:25). We are also called to intercede for others (1 Timothy 2:1).

interpretation (in-*ter*-preh-*tay*-shun)
What we believe a Bible passage means. Because the Bible was written in languages and cultures different from our own, parts of it can be hard to understand. But with the help of scholars and other people who know more than we do, we can figure those verses out.

Isaac (*eye*-zak)
Father of Jacob and Esau. Isaac was the miracle baby born to Abraham and Sarah when they were very old. Later God tested Abraham's obedience by asking him to sacrifice Isaac. Abraham was about to do it when the Angel of the Lord told him to stop — he'd passed the test. Whew!

Isaiah (eye-*zay*-ah)
A prophet from Judah who predicted Jesus' arrival hundreds of years before it happened. Isaiah's prophecies are recorded in the book of Isaiah in the Old Testament. The first half of Isaiah predicts Judah's destruction. The second half predicts the good things that will happen when Judah returns to God.

Ishmael (*ish*-mail)
The first son of Abraham, born to Hagar. Although Isaac was to be Abraham's heir, God promised that Ishmael's descendants would also grow into a mighty nation. Ishmael had twelve sons and one daughter. His descendants, the Ishmaelites, settled in northern Arabia. Many modern-day Arabs are Ishmael's descendants.

Israel (*iz*-ray-el)
1. Israel means "Prince of God." God changed Jacob's name to Israel when he promised to turn his descendants into a great nation. 2. After the Israelites conquered Canaan, the entire country was called Israel. When Israel divided into two kingdoms after Solomon's death, only the northern half was called Israel. The south was called Judah.

Israelites (*iz*-rail-ites)
The people who descended from Jacob — or Israel, as he was later known. Israelites were also called children of Israel. They were God's chosen people. Through them God restored his relationship with humankind through Jesus.

Issachar (*iss*-a-kar)
Ninth son of Jacob and father of one of Israel's twelve tribes. Jacob prophesied that Issachar's tribe would be a "strong donkey" (Genesis 49:14–15). That was a compliment, believe it or not! But Jacob also said Issachar's love of comfort would always make them take the easy way out, which would lead to trouble.

Israel *(see dictionary entry on previous page)*

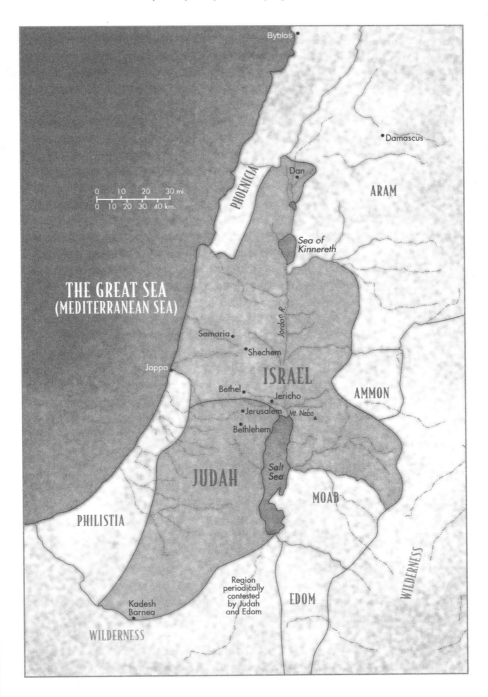

Byblos

Damascus

PHOENICIA

Dan

ARAM

Sea of
Kinnereth

THE GREAT SEA
(MEDITERRANEAN SEA)

Jordan R.

Samaria

Shechem

Joppa

ISRAEL

Bethel

Jericho

AMMON

Jerusalem

Mt. Nebo

Bethlehem

Salt
Sea

JUDAH

MOAB

PHILISTIA

WILDERNESS

Kadesh
Barnea

Region
periodically
contested
by Judah
and Edom

EDOM

WILDERNESS

0   10   20   30 mi.
0 10 20 30 40 km.

ivory (*i*-vor-ee)

White ivory comes from elephant tusks. During Bible times, ivory was a rare and expensive item that only kings and other rich people could afford. It was usually carved and inlaid in wooden furniture, such as thrones and beds.

Jacob (*jay*-cub)

A son of Isaac and Rebekah. When he was young, Jacob cheated his brother Esau out of his birthright and blessing. Esau wanted to kill Jacob, so Jacob left town. On the road, Jacob had a dream of angels on a heavenly staircase, and he promised to serve God. Years later Jacob was on his way back to see Esau when he met God and wrestled with him all night. When Jacob refused to say "uncle," God blessed him and changed his name to Israel, which means "Prince of God." Jacob had twelve sons, whose descendants became the twelve tribes of Israel.

James, brother of Jesus

Jesus' younger brother and the leader of the Jerusalem church. When Paul insisted that Gentile Christians didn't have to obey Jewish law, James sided with Paul. James also wrote a letter to Jewish believers telling them how to live. This letter is the book of James in the New Testament.

James, brother of John

A fisherman from the Sea of Galilee who became one of Jesus' first disciples. James and John were called the Sons of Thunder because they tended to fly off the handle. James was part of Jesus' inner circle, which also included Peter and John. He was the first apostle to be martyred.

Japheth (*jaf*-feth)

Noah's eldest son. After Japheth stepped off the ark, he had lots of kids with funny names. They included Gomer, Magog, and Tubal, among others. Makes you kind of thankful for *your* name, doesn't it?

jealous/jealousy (*jel*-us/*jel*-us-ee)

The feeling you sometimes get when someone you love shows devotion for someone else. Many times in the Bible, God describes himself as jealous (see Exodus 34:14). He wants his people to worship only him. Jealousy can also be a negative thing, such as when we envy people or covet their possessions.

Jehoiachin (je-*hoy*-ah-kin)
One of the last kings of Judah. Jehoiachin tried to be evil like his dad, Jehoiakim. But Jehoiachin held power for a measly three months before the Babylonians squashed his kingdom. He spent the next thirty-six years in prison.

Jehoiakim (je-*hoy*-ah-kim)
An evil king of Judah who didn't give a hoot about obeying God — unlike his father, Josiah. The prophet Jeremiah was constantly on Jehoiakim's case for the bad things he did, but Jehoiakim wouldn't listen. He started a rebellion, but his fun ended when he was carted off to Babylon as a prisoner.

Jehoshaphat (je-*hosh*-a-fat)
One of the few good kings of Judah, just like his father Asa. Jehoshaphat helped people draw closer to God by getting rid of pagan altars and sending out teachers to tell people about God. Okay, he had one fault. He got a little too chummy with Ahab, evil king of Israel.

Jehu (*jay*-who)
This king of Israel, known for his wild chariot driving, was given the job of wiping out Ahab's family. First to go was Ahab's evil wife Jezebel. Next were Ahab's seventy sons. Then his friends and advisors. Finally, *all* the worshipers of Baal. Did we also mention he was thorough?

Jepthah (*jef*-tha)
Jepthah led the Israelites in a wild and woolly battle against the Ammonites — and won! He was so happy when he won that he promised God he would sacrifice the first thing that came out of his house to meet him when he went home. That thing turned out to be his daughter.

Jeremiah (jair-e-*my*-uh)
A prophet at a time when almost no one in Judah obeyed God. (No wonder he's called the weeping prophet!) Jeremiah warned that if people didn't shape up, Babylon would attack and enslave them. They didn't, and Babylon did. Jeremiah's prophecies are in the book of Jeremiah in the Old Testament.

Jericho (*jair*-i-ko)
A city just east of Jerusalem above the Dead Sea. Jericho was the first city in Canaan that the Israelites defeated. All they did was march around the city thirteen times, blow their trumpets, give a mighty shout, and the walls came crashing down. Okay, maybe God helped out. A lot.

Jeroboam 1 (*jer*-o-*bo*-am)

The first king of the northern kingdom of Israel. When Rehoboam, Solomon's son, was too harsh on the people, the ten northern tribes of Israel revolted and made Jeroboam their king. Unfortunately Jeroboam turned around and sank Israel into centuries of idolatry.

Jeroboam 2 (*jer*-o-*bo*-am)

Jeroboam 2 was not godly, but he was a powerful warrior king who conquered a lot of land Israel had lost to its enemies. People in Israel became quite wealthy. They weren't sharing their wealth and often took advantage of the poor. So despite their victories, they were really losers.

Jerusalem (ja-*ru*-suh-lum)

The capital of Israel. Jerusalem means "possession of peace." Because Solomon built the temple on Mount Zion in Jerusalem, the city was sometimes called Zion. Over the centuries, Jerusalem was destroyed and rebuilt several times. Jesus was crucified in Jerusalem. The city was also the center for the early church.

Jesse (*jes*-see)

Father of King David and ancestor of Jesus. God sent the prophet Samuel to Bethlehem to select a king from Jesse's eight sons. To Jesse's surprise, the first seven were rejected. And the award went to . . . David! Isaiah predicted the Messiah would come from the "Root of Jesse" (Isaiah 11:10).

Jesus (*jee*-zus)

The Son of God. He is the second person of the Trinity, which also includes God the Father and the Holy Spirit. Jesus has always existed, but he came to earth as a baby around two thousand years ago. Jesus was perfect and never sinned, and when he grew up, he showed us what God was like by loving people, healing them, doing miracles, and teaching them about God. The religious leaders didn't like Jesus, so they arrested and crucified him. But this was no accident; it was prophesied that Jesus would die to pay for our sins. Three days later, he rose from the dead and appeared to his followers. Then he went up to heaven — but not before promising to return one day!

Jesus' birth (*jee*-zus')

The coming to earth of Jesus, God's son, as a baby. Jesus was born of Mary, a virgin, by the power of God's Holy Spirit. His birth is sometimes called Jesus' first coming, and Christians celebrate it on Christmas Day, December 25.

Jesus going to heaven (*jee*-zus)

After Jesus rose from the dead, he appeared to the disciples many times and taught them more about God's kingdom. After forty days, he led his disciples to the Mount of Olives, blessed them, and rose up into heaven right before their eyes!

Jesus, second coming of (*jee*-zus)

The future return of Jesus. When Jesus went up into heaven, angels said he would return again one day. But next time, he won't come as a baby. He will return as a mighty, glorious king to take us away to heaven with him forever. So keep your eye on the sky!

Jethro (*jeth*-row)

A priest of Midian who became Moses' father-in-law. Moses tended Jethro's sheep for forty years while he was hiding out from the Egyptians. Later Jethro paid Moses a visit while the Israelites were camped around Mount Sinai and gave Moses advice on how to manage his people.

Jews (juze)

Another name for the people of Israel. This name was originally used to describe people from the southern kingdom of Judah. However, after the Jews returned from captivity in Babylon, people used it to describe all Israelites.

Jezebel (*jez*-eh-bell)

The extremely wicked wife of Ahab, king of Israel. After corrupting the nation with Baal worship, Jezebel slaughtered God's priests and did all sorts of other dastardly deeds. However, her number came up when she was tossed out of a window. Let's just say the dogs ate well that night.

Jezreel Valley (*jez*-reel *val*-lee)

The valley that separates Samaria from Galilee. The Jezreel Valley was a crossroads for two major trading routes during Bible times. It was also the site of many battles, such as when Gideon and the Israelites defeated the Midianites and Amalekites (see Judges 6:33–7:25).

Joab (*joe*-ab)

David's military commander. At first Joab was a brave and trustworthy man. But then he killed Abner, Saul's military commander. After that, Joab helped David murder Uriah. Then he killed David's son Absalom, and then Amasa, the man who replaced Joab as David's commander. Any wonder that Joab was finally killed?

Joash (*joe*-ash)

1. The eighth king of Judah. He followed the Lord at first. But later on he developed an addiction to Baal that he just couldn't kick. So he got kicked by Syria instead. 2. The thirteenth king of Israel. He helped strengthen the country, but he couldn't stay away from Baal either.

Job (jobe)

A rich man in the Bible who loved God. God allowed Satan to take everything from Job—house, children, possessions, and health. Job suffered horribly, but he never rejected God. God rewarded Job's faith by giving him back twice as much as he had before. Not a bad deal.

Joel (*joe*-el)

A prophet to Judah. Joel talked a lot about locusts—locust swarms, locust plagues, great locusts, young locusts, and other locusts. He even talked about armies of locusts marching to war! Joel also talked about God pouring out his Spirit on all people.

John, the apostle (jon the uh-*pos*-ul)

A fisherman who, with his brother James, became one of Jesus' disciples. John was called "the disciple Jesus loved" (John 13:23). John went on to become a strong leader in the church. He also wrote the gospel of John; 1, 2, and 3 John, and the book of Revelation.

John the Baptist (jon the *bap*-tist)

The prophet who announced the coming of the Messiah and baptized Jesus. John looked like a wild man from the desert with his camel's-hair clothes. But people came from all over to hear him preach and be baptized by him. He was later arrested by Herod and beheaded.

Jonah (*joe*-nuh)

A prophet who tried to run from God so he wouldn't have to preach to Nineveh. He didn't get far. God sent a gigantic fish to swallow him. After three days in the fish's smelly belly, Jonah came to his senses. The fish barfed him out, and Jonah went to Nineveh (but probably not before taking a *long* bath).

Jonathan (*jon* uh-thun)
King Saul's eldest son. Jonathan was a mighty warrior prince and a loyal friend who stuck by David through thick and thin. Jonathan warned David every time Saul was out to kill him. Jonathan died a courageous, tragic death in a battle against the Philistines.

Joppa (*jop*-ah)
A city on the coast of the Mediterranean that served as a seaport for Jerusalem. Joppa was where Peter received the vision that told him the gospel was for Gentiles as well as Jews (Acts 10:9–16). Dorcas, the woman Peter brought back from the dead, lived in Joppa.

Jordan River (*jor*-dun *riv*-ver)
The longest and most important river in Israel. The Jordan was difficult to cross because it was so fast and because it flooded its banks in spring. However, God parted the Jordan so that Joshua and the Israelites could cross into Canaan. Jesus was baptized in the Jordan River by John the Baptist.

Joseph, son of Jacob (*joe*-suf)
The second-youngest son of Jacob (Israel). Joseph was Jacob's favorite son, and he gave Joseph a special coat. This made Joseph's brothers jealous, so they sold him to some merchants. Joseph stayed faithful to God, even as a slave in Egypt, but he was falsely accused and ended up in prison. Years later, God helped Joseph explain a dream to Pharaoh, the king of Egypt. He told the king that a huge famine was coming! Joseph then was put in charge of Egypt to help prepare for the famine. When Joseph's family visited him, Joseph forgave his brothers and invited everyone to live in Egypt.

Joseph, husband of Mary (*joe*-suf)
Joseph helped rear Jesus, but he wasn't Jesus' father. *God* was. When Joseph found out his fiancée Mary was pregnant, he considered stopping the marriage, but an angel told him to hold his horses. This baby was from God, not some other guy. So Joseph married Mary.

Joshua (*josh*-you-uh)
Moses' right-hand man and one of the twelve spies he sent into Canaan. Joshua believed they could beat the Canaanites, but the Israelites refused to believe. Result? They wandered in the wilderness for forty years. Later Joshua got his chance to lead the Israelites into Canaan and conquer the land.

Josiah (joe-*zi*-ah)
The sixteenth king of Judah. Josiah was a good king who cleared the idols from Judah and repaired the temple. That's when someone rediscovered the scroll of the Law. When Josiah read it, he was horrified at how far Judah had slipped from God. He worked even harder to get his country back on track.

Jotham (*joe*-tham)
1. Eleventh king of Judah, the son of Uzziah. Jotham was faithful to God throughout his life. Of course, he had a little help from some prophetic friends: Isaiah, Hosea, and Micah. 2. Gideon's youngest son, a parable teller who escaped from the murderous Abimelech (Judges 9:1–21).

joy
A lasting happiness that comes from the Holy Spirit. Human happiness comes and goes depending on what's happening. But joy is a deep, cheerful feeling that sticks with us no matter what. Being joyful doesn't mean always being happy. It means being content because you know God is caring for you.

Jubilee. See *Year of Jubilee.* (jew-ba-*lee*)

Judah (*jew*-duh)
1. One of the twelve sons of Jacob (Israel). 2. The tribe descended from Judah. King David came from this tribe. So did Jesus. 3. The area of land given to the tribe of Judah. 4. The name of the southern kingdom when Israel divided into two parts after Solomon's death.

Judas Iscariot (*jew*-dus is-*care*-ee-ut)
The man who betrayed Jesus. He believed Jesus was the Messiah. But when Jesus didn't rally the troops to give the Romans the boot, Judas betrayed him to the Jewish religious leaders for thirty silver coins. Afterward, Judas felt so guilty about what he'd done he hanged himself.

Judea (ju-*day*-ah)
The Greek and Roman name for the kingdom of Judah. After the Babylonians conquered Judah, it became a province of the Persian Empire. Then it became a part of the Grecian empire. Then it was independent for a while. Then it was taken over by Herod. Then by the Romans. Poor Judea!

judge (judj)
Military leaders God raised up to help the Israelites defeat their enemies. The judges ruled for centuries, from the death of Joshua until Saul became king. Famous judges include Samson, Gideon, Deborah, and Ehud. Their stories are in the book of Judges in the Old Testament.

Judgment Day (*judj*-munt day)
The time when Jesus, with the authority of God the Father, judges the entire world. The righteous — those who trust Jesus and are saved — will be judged and rewarded (2 Corinthians 5:10), and the unrighteous will be judged for their evil deeds and sent to the lake of fire (Revelation 20:11–15).

justice (*jus*-tiss)
Punishing evil and rewarding righteousness. Justice also means treating everyone fairly, as God treats us. In Bible times, poor people were often mistreated in court, because they couldn't afford to bribe the judge like the rich people could. Many Old Testament prophets preached against this.

kindness (*kind*-nuss)
Being pleasant, helpful, and considerate of people, no matter who they are. Kindness is a fruit of the Spirit. We should be kind to everyone, because God has shown us the ultimate kindness: forgiving us for our sins. Hey, and he did it even while we were his enemies (Romans 5:10)!

king
The royal leader of a kingdom. God was the king of Israel, but the Israelites wanted a human leader — a flesh-and-blood king. God warned them against this desire, but they insisted. Their first king, Saul, wasn't so good. David was better. But God is still the King of Kings (1 Timothy 6:15).

kingdom (*king*-dum)
A nation or land ruled by a king. Once God gave the Israelites a human king, their nation became known as the kingdom of Israel. Many other huge kingdoms or empires appear in the Bible, such as the kingdoms of Babylon, Assyria, and Egypt.

kingdom of God (*king*-dum uv god)
The kingdom of God (also called the kingdom of heaven) is more than just a nation or city ruled by a king. It's a spiritual kingdom that includes everyone in heaven and on earth who knows God. If you're a Christian, you're living in God's kingdom right now!

kiss

It was common in Bible times for relatives or close friends to kiss each other on the cheek when they met or when they parted company. Judas betrayed Jesus with this type of kiss (Luke 22:47–48).

knowledge (*nol*-idge)

Awareness and understanding of people, places, things, and ideas. Knowledge is good, but without wisdom to show you how to use it, it's useless. Respect for God is the beginning of *all* knowledge and wisdom (Proverbs 1:3). So if you want knowledge, you know whom to ask!

Korah (*kor*-ah)

A Levite who rebelled against Moses' and Aaron's leadership. Rather than fight, Moses let God decide who should be in charge. God answered by ripping open the earth, swallowing Korah and his men in an earthquake, and burning the rest of his followers (Numbers 16). Anyone *else* want to be boss?

L

Laban (*lay*-ban)

Jacob's father-in-law and a *real* shifty fellow. First he made Jacob work seven years before he could marry Rachel, Laban's younger daughter. Then Laban tricked Jacob by giving him his elder daughter Leah instead! Jacob had to work seven *more* years before he could marry Rachel. Would *you* want Laban for a father-in-law?

Lamb, Passover (lam, *pass*-o-ver)

When the Israelites were slaves in Egypt, God told them to kill a lamb and smear its blood on their doorposts so God's angel would "pass over" them and not kill their firstborn son (Exodus 12). For centuries afterward, the Israelites sacrificed a lamb on Passover. Jesus was the ultimate Passover Lamb.

lamp

An oil-burning clay or metal vessel used for light. Lamps were usually quite simple—they had a hole for putting oil in and a hole for the wick. They stayed lit for about four hours. Over time, the lamp became a symbol for understanding, guidance, and life.

law

Rules that say how a society should work. Laws state which behaviors a society accepts and which it doesn't. They also include punishments for people who break the law. Paul wrote in Romans 13 that God wants Christians to obey the laws of the land.

Law of Moses, the

Rules and regulations for how the Israelites were to live. God gave the Ten Commandments to Moses on Mount Sinai. The Law included the Ten Commandments and oodles of other rules about worship, food, and morals. Only problem was, these laws were tough, and it was impossible to keep them all. And if you broke just one, you were guilty of breaking them all! *Great!* So why did God give the Law? So people could see they were sinful and needed salvation. Then God sent his son Jesus to save us and to set us free from the Law (Galatians 3:19). Thank God!

Lazarus (*laz*-a-rus)

1. A man Jesus brought back from the dead (John 11:1–45). Lazarus was Jesus' friend and the brother of Mary and Martha, two of Jesus' followers.
2. A poor beggar in one of Jesus' parables (Luke 16:19–31). He went to heaven while the rich man went . . . somewhere else.

lazy/laziness (*lay*-zee/*lay*-zee-nuss)

An attitude that makes you want to sit around like a half-dead sloth rather than work. If you want to be poor, unhappy, and despised by everyone, then a life of laziness is for you. But if you want to be happy, healthy, wealthy, and wise, get off the couch and exercise!

learning (*ler*-ning)

The process of discovering and understanding new things. Some learning happens in school by reading books and listening to teachers. Other learning happens in the school of life experience. Wise people always want to learn new things.

Lebanon (*leb*-a-non)

1. A mountain range in Syria. It was the northern border of the Promised Land.
2. A nation during Bible times famous for its beautiful landscape and lush vegetation — especially its majestic cedar trees. Lebanon still exists today, but its great forests are almost completely gone.

legion (*lee*-gin)
The main unit in the Roman army. A legion was made up of between three thousand and six thousand foot soldiers and one hundred to two hundred soldiers on horseback. The New Testament uses the word *legion* to describe any great number — like we use the word *kazillion* today (see Mark 5:9).

leper/leprosy (*le*-per/*le*-pro-see)
A terrible, incurable skin disease. People who had leprosy during Bible times had to live in separate communities so they wouldn't infect others. Elisha miraculously healed Naaman, an Assyrian general, of leprosy (2 Kings 5). Jesus also showed God's power by healing lepers (Luke 17:11–19).

Levi (*leev*-eye)
Jacob's son and father of one of the twelve tribes of Israel. It's a wonder that Levi's descendants became Israel's priests, because Levi definitely wasn't a model citizen. He and his brother Simeon played a dirty trick on some guys and then killed them (Genesis 34). Maybe he reformed later in life.

Leviathan (lev-*eye*-a-thin)
A crocodile, giant serpent, or some sort of sea monster. Leviathan is described different ways in the Bible, making it difficult to figure out exactly what kind of creature it was (see Job 41; Psalm 104:26). One thing is for sure: you *don't* want to mess with one!

Levites (*lee*-vites)
Descendants of Levi, one of the sons of Israel. Starting with Aaron, God set aside the Levite tribe as the priests of Israel. They were in charge of the holy tent and the temple. They also led the Israelites in their worship of God.

lie/lying
Saying something you know is not true. You should always tell the truth because God is truth and he wants you to be like him. Sometimes it seems like a little lie will save you from a lot of trouble. Wrong. Lies only lead to more lies.

life, eternal (life e-*ter*-nul)
Never-ending life, the reward for those who trust in Jesus. If you think *this* life is good, just wait until you get to heaven! There you'll get a new body that will last forever and ever and ever and can do cool things (Luke 24:36–37)!

lion (*lie*-un)

A large, dangerous member of the cat family. Famous lions include the one David killed with his sling, the one Samson killed with his bare hands, and the ones Daniel spent the night with (Daniel 6). But the most famous lion of all is Jesus: the "Lion of the tribe of Judah" (Revelation 5:5).

locust (*low*-kist)

An insect similar to a grasshopper. When a swarm of locusts comes to town, you might as well kiss your crops good-bye, because they'll devour every plant in sight. The eighth plague God sent upon Egypt was a locust swarm. Some people in the Bible ate locusts (Matthew 3:4).

Lord

1. A ruler who owns people or things. We call Jesus Lord because he is our Master, and we belong to him. 2. The word LORD (in small capital letters) is also used in the Old Testament whenever God's name, Yahweh, appears. See *Yahweh.*

Lord's Day

In the Bible, the Sabbath was celebrated every Saturday. It was the day of rest. Today Christians celebrate Sunday as the Lord's Day because that's the day of the week Jesus rose from the dead. In Acts, Christians met on Sunday and worshiped God. We follow their example today.

Lord's Prayer

A prayer outline that Jesus gave his disciples (Matthew 6:5–15). According to this outline, you should begin each prayer by addressing God personally. Next you should praise him. Then you should pray for God's kingdom to grow and for his will to be done everywhere (especially in *your* life). Next ask God to provide for your needs. Then ask him to forgive your sins and help you forgive others. Finally, ask God to help you obey him. There you have it. Next time you don't know how to pray, just stick to this outline and you won't go wrong!

Lord's Supper

The ceremony that celebrates Jesus' death for our sins. It is also called Communion or the Eucharist. Jesus celebrated this the night before he died. After he and his disciples ate the Passover meal, he broke the bread and passed a piece to each person. He said it stood for his body, which would be broken for them. Then he passed around the wine. He told them it stood for his blood, which would be shed for them. Jesus said we should continue to do this in remembrance of his sacrifice for us (Luke 22:1–20).

Lot

Abraham's nephew who traveled to Canaan with him. After they split up, Lot moved to Sodom, an evil city. Dumb move. He and his family barely escaped with their lives, and his wife was turned to *salt* (Genesis 19:1–26). Lot later fathered two children through his daughters while he was drunk. Lot made a lot of mistakes.

lots. See *casting lots.*

love (luv)

A strong feeling of liking and accepting someone. Love also makes you want to do what's best for others. The two greatest commandments in the Bible are to love God and to love others (Matthew 22:37–39). We are to be loving, because God *is* love (1 John 4:8). He loves us so much that he gave up his only son Jesus so we could be saved from our sins. For a full-on description of what love is all about, read what Paul wrote in 1 Corinthians 13. This kind of love is amazing, and it's a gift of the Holy Spirit.

Luke

A doctor who traveled with the apostle Paul and helped him preach the gospel. Luke wrote two long books in the New Testament: the gospel of Luke and the Acts of the Apostles. The gospel of Luke was written so Gentiles could understand who Jesus was. Acts is an exciting history of the early church.

made fun of

Sometimes kids may tease you or call you names because you're a Christian or because you choose to do what's right. That can hurt, but Jesus said not to try and get even when people persecute you. Love them and pray for them instead (Matthew 5:44).

magic *(ma-jik)*

Activities such as fortune-telling, witchcraft, and speaking with the dead. Magic is forbidden by God because it involves evil spirits (Deuteronomy 18:9–10). This doesn't mean you can't have a magician at your next birthday party. That kind of magician merely does illusions — tricks that fool the eye.

Manasseh, son of Joseph *(man-ah-sah)*

Joseph's firstborn son. Manasseh and his brother, Ephraim, were adopted by their grandfather Jacob (Israel). Jacob did this because he had disinherited his eldest son, Reuben, for sinning against him. Manasseh and Ephraim each fathered one of the twelve tribes of Israel.

Manasseh, king of Judah *(man-ah-sah)*

The longest-reigning, most evil king Judah ever had. Manasseh worshiped everything that moved — except God. He tried to reform late in life, but his son Amon quickly put a stop to it. Seems he learned a thing or two from watching daddy. Too bad Manasseh hadn't learned from *his* daddy, good king Hezekiah.

Manasseh, tribe of *(man-ah-sah)*

One of the twelve tribes of Israel at the time the land of Canaan was divided between Jacob's descendants. The tribe of Manasseh descended from Joseph's eldest son, Manasseh, the adopted son of Jacob (Israel). The tribe of Manasseh was known for its military strength. Two judges came from Manasseh: Gideon and Jephthah.

manger *(mane-jer)*

A feeding trough used in stables to feed animals. Jesus was placed in a manger after he was born (Luke 2:7). Mangers usually held hay, not slop. (Baby Jesus was probably thankful for that!) Most nativity scenes show a wooden manger, but mangers were actually made of clay or stone.

manna (*man*-ah)
The food God miraculously provided for the Israelites in the wilderness (Exodus 16). Each morning, the ground around the Israelite camp was white with flakes that looked like frost. This sweet stuff could be ground into flour, then baked, boiled, or cooked into cakes. Yum!

Mark
Barnabas's cousin. Mark went on a missionary trip with Paul and Barnabas but turned back not far into it. After that, Paul refused to travel with Mark again. Years later he and Mark hugged, made up, and then worked together again. Mark also wrote the gospel of Mark with help from Peter.

mark of the Beast (beest)
A stamp or some evil mark that the Antichrist will force people to receive on their right hands or foreheads (Revelation 13:16–17). This type of mark was used in Bible times to identify slaves with their masters. Anyone who takes the mark of the Beast will become the Antichrist's slave.

marriage (*mare*-ridg)
The joining of a man and woman as husband and wife. This is God's plan for creating families. When people get married, they promise to love and be faithful to each other until death. This is *the* most important promise a man and a woman can make to each other.

Martha (*mar*-tha)
Sister of Mary and Lazarus. Martha was always bustling around trying to look after Jesus' needs. When her sister, Mary, sat on the floor listening to Jesus teach, Martha got on Mary's case. But Martha was also a very spiritual lady who had deep talks with Jesus (see John 11:20–27).

martyr (*mar*-ter)

Someone who dies for his or her faith. Martyr originally meant "witness." When early Christians were suffering and being persecuted and killed for witnessing about Jesus, they were described as martyrs. People are still martyred for their faith today.

Mary, mother of Jesus (*mare*-ee)

A young woman from the town of Nazareth in Galilee. While Mary was engaged to Joseph, the angel Gabriel announced that she would become pregnant by the Holy Spirit and give birth to the Messiah. Wouldn't that rock your world? Mary took it all in stride and gave birth to Jesus in Bethlehem.

Mary of Bethany (*mare*-ee of *beth*-an-ee)

Sister of Martha and Lazarus. Unlike her sister, Martha, who was always working, Mary spent as much time as possible learning from Jesus. She also anointed Jesus' feet with expensive perfume shortly before he died (John 12:1–8). She was criticized for doing that, but Jesus defended and praised her.

Mary Magdalene (*mare*-ee *mag*-duh-leen)

A woman out of whom Jesus drove seven demons. Mary Magdalene followed Jesus closely throughout his ministry. She, along with Jesus' mother, was present at Jesus' crucifixion. Mary Magdalene was also the first person to see Jesus after he rose from the dead (Mark 16:9). What a privilege!

Matthew (*ma*-thew)

A tax collector who became one of the twelve apostles. It took only two words from Jesus and Matthew jumped up from his desk, threw a big feast for Jesus, and then followed him (Matthew 9:9–10). Matthew wrote the gospel of Matthew to show the Jews that Jesus was the Messiah.

Mediterranean Sea (med-i-ter-*ane*-ee-un)

A large sea that borders Israel and other nations of the Bible, such as Egypt and Lebanon. The Bible also calls the Mediterranean the "Great Sea." The Romans called it *Mare Nostrum* ("Our Sea"). The Mediterranean was an important trade route during Bible times. Paul often sailed on it during his missionary journeys.

Medo-Persia (*mee*-do *perz*-uh)

After Persia and Media conquered Assyria, they united to form one empire. The two nations had a sort of seesaw, power-sharing arrangement, where one of them ruled, then the other. Cyrus, a Persian, ruled this empire at the height of its power. Cyrus let the Jews who were prisoners in Babylon go back to their land and rebuild Jerusalem.

Melchizedek (mel-*kiz*-i-dek)

The king of Salem (Jerusalem) and a priest of "God Most High" (Genesis 14:18–20). Melchizedek appeared one moment and disappeared the next. *Very* mysterious. As priest and king, Melchizedek was a model for what Jesus was to become for us (Hebrews 6:20).

mercy (*mer*-see)

Giving people something even though they don't deserve it. God has shown incredible mercy by forgiving us for our sins and welcoming us into his family. He also shows us mercy by loving us and answering our prayers. God wants us to show mercy to others.

Messiah (mes-*eye*-ah)

A Hebrew word that means "Anointed One." It is similar to the Greek word *Christ.* The Jewish people thought the Messiah would be a mighty warrior who would set their country free from the Romans. But Jesus came to conquer by dying, not killing. That really messed with people's heads.

Methuselah (me-*thooze*-eh-lah)

Son of Enoch and father of Noah. His biggest claim to fame is that he lived longer than anyone else recorded in the Bible — a whopping 969 years! We don't know much about what he did during that time except that he had his first child at age 187.

Michael (*my*-cull)

A high-ranking angel or archangel who looked out for Israel. The book of Daniel says Michael battled the prince (fallen angel) of Persia who was working for Satan (Daniel 10:13). Michael will also lead the angels against Satan and his angels in the last days (Revelation 12:7–9).

Midian/Midianite (*mid*-ee-un/*mid*-ee-un-ite)

One of six sons Abraham had with his concubine Keturah. Midian is the ancestor of the Midianites, a tribe that was friendly to Moses but later were enemies of the Israelites. Joseph was sold to Midianite slave traders (Genesis 37:25–36), and Gideon defeated the Midianites in battle (Judges 7).

Millennium, the (mill-en-ee-um)

The thousand-year period of peace during which Jesus will rule the earth as King of Kings (Revelation 20). No one's exactly sure how this will happen, but you can be certain that when Jesus does return, he will be taking charge in a major way.

millstone (*mill*-stone)
A large, heavy, circular stone used for grinding grain into flour. Each flour mill used two millstones, one on top of the other. The top stone was turned, and lots of grain was ground between them. Women could grind small amounts of grain in bowls, but it took oxen to turn heavy millstones.

mind
Your thoughts and attitudes. God gave us brains because he wants us to use them. (Think about *that*.) Our minds gather information, make decisions, and solve problems. God also wants us to love him with our minds (Matthew 22:37–38). This means filling our thoughts with his words and wisdom.

miracle (*mir*-uh-cull)
An amazing event that bends the laws of nature. In the Bible, God did many miracles through people like prophets and apostles. Jesus did more miracles than anyone else. He performed miracles to show us God's power and love and prove that he was the Messiah.

Miriam (*mir*-ee-um)
Moses' and Aaron's older sister. Miriam grew up to be a famous prophetess (Exodus 15:20). She also made a famous mistake! She and Aaron rebelled against Moses, and God punished her by giving her leprosy. Good thing Moses prayed and God healed her.

Moab/Moabites (*mo*-ab)
1. The son of Lot and his elder daughter. Moab was the founder of the Moabite nation. They clashed with Israel throughout its history. (Read Judges 3, for example.) 2. The land east of the Dead Sea occupied by the Moabites.

money (*mun*-ee)
Something you use to buy things you need, find out how much something is worth, and measure how wealthy you are. Money can be good — can you imagine buying and selling things *without* it? — but you should never put your trust in money, only in God (Matthew 6:19–21).

Mordecai (*more*-di-kie)
Esther's cousin, who adopted her. Mordecai got in hot water for staying loyal to God and refusing to bow to Haman, the king of Persia's right-hand man. Haman tried to have Mordecai and the Jews killed, but after Esther messed up Haman's plans, Haman was killed instead and Mordecai got Haman's job.

Moses (*mo*-zuz)

The man God chose to lead the Israelites out of slavery in Egypt. Moses was born a Hebrew slave, but he was adopted by Pharaoh's daughter and became an Egyptian prince. Forty years later, he lost his cool, killed an Egyptian taskmaster, and then split for the desert. Many years later, God appeared to Moses in a burning bush and told him to lead his people out of Egypt. Together with his brother Aaron, Moses performed some powerful miracles that forced Pharaoh to send the Israelites packing. Then God used Moses to give the Israelites the Law.

Mosaic Law. See *Law of Moses, the.* (moz-ay-ik)

most important stone. See *cornerstone.*

Mount of Olives (*ol*-ivs)

A large hill east of Jerusalem. Jesus often went to the Mount of Olives to pray with his disciples. After his resurrection, Jesus rose up to heaven from the Mount of Olives. When he returns from heaven, he'll land on that same mountain and split it in two (Zechariah 14:4)!

mourning (*mor*-ning)

An expression of deep grief, especially for someone who has died. When people in the Bible mourned, they *really* got into it. They tore their clothes, wailed at the top of their lungs, and threw dust and ashes on their heads. Sometimes they even hired people to help them mourn.

music (*mu*-zik)

People in Bible times played music to celebrate victories and special events, to mourn, or to entertain themselves. Back then, they couldn't buy a CD by their favorite artist. The only music they heard was what they made themselves with harps, flutes, zithers, cymbals, and trumpets.

myrrh (*mur*)

A sweet-smelling, sticky substance used for perfume and for preparing dead bodies for burial. It was also mixed with oil for anointing people. Myrrh was quite valuable during Bible times. That's why one of the Magi brought it as a gift for baby Jesus (Matthew 2:11).

Naaman (*nay*-min)

A Syrian commander cured of leprosy. The cure was a little strange. Elisha told Naaman to dunk himself in the muddy Jordan River seven times. Naaman was too proud to do it at first, but his servants convinced him to go for it. Good thing, because God cured him!

Naboth (*nay*-both)

An Israelite who refused to sell his vineyard to King Ahab and wound up getting stoned with rocks. It was all thanks to Ahab's wife Jezebel who paid some men to accuse Naboth of blaspheming God. For that, Elijah told Ahab that he and Jezebel were through.

Naomi (na-*oh*-me)

Ruth's mother-in-law. After Naomi's and Ruth's husbands died in Moab, Ruth followed Naomi back to her hometown of Bethlehem. There Naomi acted as a matchmaker for Ruth and Boaz, a wealthy farmer. After they married, Ruth gave birth to Obed, who became an ancestor of Jesus.

Naphtali (*naff*-tha-lie)

Jacob's sixth son and father of one of the twelve tribes of Israel. Naphtali's name means "my wrestling." Born to Rachel's maid Bilhah, Rachel named him this because Naphtali's birth meant she had finally scored a point in the wrestling match she'd been fighting with her sister over who could have the most kids.

nard

An expensive, sweet-smelling oil from India used as a perfume. Mary Magdalene anointed Jesus with nard the week before he was crucified. Some of the disciples were angry, thinking it was a waste of money, but Jesus told them she had done the right thing (John 12:1–8).

Nathan (*nay*-than)

A prophet to Israel while David and Solomon ruled. At first Nathan agreed to David's plan to build the temple. He changed his mind after hearing from God. Later Nathan rebuked David for committing adultery with Bathsheba. Nathan also helped make sure Solomon became the next king.

Nazareth (*naz*-a-reth)

A town in Galilee. Although Jesus was born in Bethlehem, he grew up in Nazareth, Joseph's and Mary's hometown. Most Jews didn't think much of the place. Nathaniel, one of Jesus' followers, wondered how anything good could come from there (John 1:46). Well, you just *watch*, Nate!

Nazirite (*naz*-er-ite)

A person who sets himself or herself apart from the world in order to draw closer to God. People usually became Nazirites for a month or two. But some people, such as Samson, were Nazirites for life. Nazirites could not cut their hair, drink wine, or touch a dead body (Numbers 6:1–8).

Nebuchadnezzar (*neb*-you-kad-*nez*-er)

The king of Babylon who flattened Jerusalem and took nearly everyone in Judah as prisoners. Nebuchadnezzar was also the guy who threw Daniel's friends into the fiery furnace. God later humbled Nebuchadnezzar by making him live and eat like an animal (Daniel 4:29–37). After that experience, Neb became a believer.

Negev, the (*neg*-ev)

A dry, desert-like wilderness in southern Judah. Abraham and Isaac lived in the Negev for a time, and Joshua and the spies entered the Promised Land from there. Important trade routes passed through this region, so Solomon and Uzziah built many fortresses in the area.

Nehemiah (knee-uh-*my*-uh)

A Jewish high official in the Persian court. After the Jews returned to Judah, Nehemiah left Babylon to lead them in rebuilding the walls around Jerusalem. Some of his enemies tried to stop him, but God helped Nehemiah and his crew finish the job. His story is found in the book of Nehemiah.

Nero (*knee*-row)

The fifth emperor of Rome. Nero set Rome on fire and then blamed the Christians. This started a terrible persecution in which many believers were killed — including Peter and Paul. Nero's personal life was so scandalous that noble Romans told him to kill himself. He eventually took their advice.

New Moon Festival (nu moon *fes*-ti-vul)

A feast day to celebrate the beginning of each month when the new moon arrived. Many ancient cultures celebrated this event. The Israelite celebration involved giving additional offerings to make up for any extra sins that were committed the month before. Then people could start out the new month fresh.

Nicodemus (nick-o-*dee*-mus)

A Pharisee who recognized that Jesus was from God. When Nicodemus asked Jesus if he was the Messiah, Jesus told him about being born again (John 3:3). Nicodemus must have gone for it later on, because he defended Jesus in front of the Sanhedrin and helped with Jesus' burial.

Nile River

The longest (and only) river in Egypt. The Nile was the lifeblood of Egypt, because the rest of the country was nothing but desert. It provided water for crops and was the main transportation route. As a baby, Moses was set afloat in the Nile (Exodus 2:1–5).

Nineveh (*nin*-e-vah)

The capital of Assyria. Nineveh was where Jonah preached after trying to run away from God. After hearing Jonah, the Ninevites sincerely repented. But it didn't last long. Nahum predicted Nineveh would be destroyed for its wickedness (Nahum 2:1–3:19; in 612 B.C.). It was.

oath

A promise made before God. Oaths contained a promise or a curse or a request for God to punish the oath maker if he didn't keep his promise. By Jesus' day, people were making silly oaths, swearing by their heads and the gold in the temple (see Matthew 5:33–37; 23:16).

Obadiah (o-ba-*die*-ah)

1. A godly official in Ahab's court who hid one hundred prophets of God while Jezebel was trying to wipe them out. 2. A prophet of Judah. He spoke out against Edom for taking sides against Jerusalem and predicted that Edom would soon be destroyed. His prophecies are in the book of Obadiah.

obey (o-*bay*)

To do what you are told. God wants you to obey him because he loves you and knows what's best for you. The same goes for your parents. They only give you rules to obey because they want what's best for you. Believe it or not!

offering (*off*-er-ing)

Something given to God as an act of worship or as payment for sin. In the Old Testament, offerings could be anything from animals to crops or drinks. Today we usually use the word offering to refer to the money we give (offer) to church. See *sacrifice*.

Og

King of the Amorites and last surviving member of a race of giants. Og was defeated by Moses and the Israelites when they came out of the wilderness. This humongous brute is known for having the largest bed in the Bible. It was thirteen feet long and six feet wide (Deuteronomy 3:11)!

oil (oyl)

A thick liquid made from olives, berries, or fruit. Oil was important during Bible times. It was used for cooking, cosmetics, medicine, preparing bodies for burial, and burning in lamps. Oil was also used for religious purposes, such as anointing people and making offerings.

oldest son

In Bible times, firstborn sons received the birthright or blessing from their fathers. This blessing included a double portion of their father's land, money, and other belongings. The oldest son also became the new head of the family. You oldest sons probably wish we still did that today!

olive (*all*-iv)

A fruit shaped like a tiny egg. During Bible times, olives were eaten fresh or pressed into oil. They grew in orchards and were harvested by whacking their tree branches with a stick. The Mount of Olives, where Jesus and his disciples often hung out, was covered with olive trees.

ordain (or-*dain*)

To officially send someone out to serve God. In Bible times, this was usually done by laying hands on people and praying for them (Acts 6:1–7). Today we ordain ministers and pastors in special ceremonies. These ceremonies also involve prayer and the laying on of hands.

orthodox (*or*-tho-docks)

Something that lines up with what is true. The word *orthodox* is usually used to describe religious beliefs or teachings. Churches that agree with the main teaching of Christianity, such as the Apostles' Creed, are orthodox. Those that don't are called unorthodox.

Othniel (*oth*-kneel)

The first judge of Israel. After Joshua died, the Israelites turned away from God and worshiped Canaanite gods. God punished them by letting a king of Mesopotamia conquer them. When they repented and cried out to God, he had Othniel lead them in battle and defeat their enemies.

oxen (*ox*-un)

Large, chunky cattle. Oxen were important animals during Bible times. They were used for food, to pull carts or ploughs, and as offerings to God. Wealth was also measured by how many oxen you had. Oxen were so large you had to be rich just to be able to feed them!

P

Palestine (*pal*-luh-stine)
After the Israelites conquered the land of Canaan, they named it Israel. In New Testament times, their lands were called Judea and Galilee. After the Jews waged war against Rome in 132–135 A.D., the Romans kicked them all out of their country and renamed it Palestine (after the Philistines).

palm
Tall trees that have a large spread of leaves growing at the top. Palm trees grew all over Bible lands, and travelers were always glad to see them because they meant water and shade were nearby. When Jesus entered Jerusalem, people waved palm branches to proclaim him king (John 12:13).

papyrus (pa-*pie*-rus)
A tall, grass-like plant that grows in shallow water along rivers and lakes. Papyrus was used to make paper. The stalks of the plants were cut into strips, then pounded and pressed into sheets and dried in the sun. Much of the Old Testament was written on papyrus.

parable See *story*. (*pair*-uh-bull)

paradise (*pair*-uh-dice)
A Persian word that means "park" or "orchard." The Bible uses "paradise" to describe any perfect place, such as the Garden of Eden or heaven. When Jesus was on the cross, he told the thief beside him that he would be with him in paradise that day (Luke 23:43).

parchment (*parch*-munt)
A writing material made from the skins of sheep, goats, or cattle. The skins were specially prepared like leather, sewn into long sheets, and rolled up into scrolls. It was quite an honor, really, for a goat to have a scribe write the Scriptures on its skin.

parents (*pair*-unts)
Mothers and fathers. God has given us parents to take care of us as we grow up. They are also in charge of teaching us about life and helping us grow in our relationship with God. Obeying your parents is one of God's top ten rules (Exodus 20:12). See also *talking back*.

Passover (*pass*-o-ver)
The greatest of all Jewish feasts. It was first celebrated in Egypt when Jewish families killed a lamb and put its blood on their doorframes. They did this so God's angel would "pass over" their house without killing their eldest sons. Many years later, Jesus died during Passover as *our* Passover Lamb.

pastor (*pass*-ter)
The leader of a church. Pastor means "shepherd" in Greek. Church leaders are called pastors because they shepherd God's flock. Pastors spend many years studying the Bible and getting to know God. Then they stay busy helping others do the same thing. Need help? Just ask your pastor. That's why he or she is there!

pasture (*past*-cher)
An open, grassy field where cattle, sheep, and other livestock eat. Today we have fences around our pastures. In Bible times, shepherds had to roam with their animals to keep track of them, help them find water, and protect them from wild animals or thieves. Sound like a fun job?

patience (*pay*-shuns)
The ability to wait for something without getting upset. Patience is a fruit of the Spirit. It helps you stay calm when facing difficulties — or difficult people. Being patient is easy if you remember that God is being patient with you right now. Just pass it on to others!

Paul (pall)
A Pharisee who persecuted Jesus' followers until he met Jesus. Paul's name used to be Saul. When Saul was traveling to Damascus to arrest Christians, Jesus appeared to him in a vision (Acts 9). After that, Saul was a changed man. (He even got a new name!) Paul went everywhere and did everything he could to spread the gospel, especially to the Gentiles. He went on three missionary journeys and started several churches. Paul also wrote many books in the New Testament, including Romans, 1 and 2 Corinthians, Galatians, and others. Talk about a changed life!

peace (piece)
A sense of calm and relaxation that comes from trusting God and knowing he is in control. Peace also means not being in conflict with anyone, including God. If you know Jesus, you can have peace, because Jesus is called the Prince of Peace (Isaiah 9:6). So just relax!

pearl (perl)

Round, precious stones made by oysters that are trying to stop a grain of sand from itching them. Pearls were valuable during Bible times, just as they are today. Jesus compared the kingdom of heaven with a precious pearl (Matthew 13:45–46). There will also be giant pearls in heaven (Revelation 21:21).

peer pressure See *pleasing people.*

Pentecost (*pen*-tuh-cost)

A Jewish feast that celebrated the beginning of harvest. (See *Feast of Harvest.*) Pentecost took place seven weeks (forty-nine days) after Passover. Pentecost means "the fiftieth day." Pentecost is an important day for Christians because that was when the Holy Spirit came to live in all believers (Acts 2).

perfume (*per*-fume)

A pleasant-smelling liquid made from herbs and other plants. Perfume was very important in Bible lands. The hot climate often made people sweaty, and perfume helped cover the smell. Perfume was also used for worship and for preparing corpses for burial.

persecution (per-se-*cue*-shun)

When people are harassed, tortured, or killed because of who they are or what they believe. Shortly after the early church started, Christians everywhere were on the run as the Pharisees, Sadducees, and Romans tried to stop Christianity. Christians are still persecuted in many countries today.

persecutions, imperial
(per-se-*cue*-shuns, im-*peer*-e-ul)

The many times Roman emperors persecuted the church. Nero was the first Caesar to persecute Christians. After Nero's time, laws were passed making it illegal to be a Christian, and a long string of Caesars tortured and executed Christians or forced them to fight lions and gladiators.

perseverance See *standing firm.* (per-su-*veer*-uns)

Persians (purr-shuns)

A powerful people in Old Testament times. (See *Medo-Persia.*) The Persian king Cyrus the Great let the Jews return home to rebuild their temple. Other Persian kings sent Ezra and Nehemiah to Jerusalem to help their people. Later Esther married a Persian king.

Peter (*pee*-ter)

A fisherman who became one of Jesus' disciples and closest friends. Peter loved Jesus, but he was also a bit of a hothead: he didn't always engage his brain before he opened his mouth. On the night before Jesus' crucifixion, Peter insisted he loved Jesus and would never forsake him. A few hours later, he pretended they'd never met. Jesus knew that deep down inside Peter was sorry for what he had said. Jesus not only forgave Peter but also made him an important leader in the early church. Peter preached in many places, including Rome. Two of his letters, 1 and 2 Peter, are in the New Testament.

Pharaoh (*fair*-oh)
The title of the kings of ancient Egypt. Abraham got in trouble with one pharaoh for pretending Sarah was his sister. Another pharaoh made Joseph the ruler of Egypt. Still another pharaoh made the Israelites slaves. Every pharaoh claimed to be a god. Funny thing, though — they all died!

Pharisees (*fair*-ih-sees)
Jewish religious leaders who were obsessed with keeping God's law — and their own laws. Problem was the Pharisees loved law keeping so much that they forgot about loving God and others. They became angry when Jesus pointed this out to them, and they plotted to kill him. Talk about touchy!

Philip the apostle (*fill*-up)
One of Jesus' twelve disciples. After Jesus invited Philip to follow him from Bethsaida to Galilee, Philip ran and invited his friend Nathaniel to come too. Philip spoke excellent Greek and is known for bringing Gentiles to Jesus (John 12:20–23). Hey! This guy *really* liked introducing people to Jesus!

Philip the evangelist (*fill*-up)
One of seven men the apostles chose to serve tables in Jerusalem. Philip is famous for sharing the gospel with the Ethiopian eunuch and then being miraculously whisked away by God (Acts 8:26–40). Philip later had four daughters who prophesied.

Philippi (fih-*lip*-eye)
A city in Macedonia where Paul and Silas were beaten and thrown into jail after Paul cast an evil spirit out of a slave girl. That night, an earthquake broke them free. Instead of running off, Paul converted the jailer! The book of Philippians is written to believers in Philippi.

Philistine (*fill*-i-steen)
Warlike people who settled on the Mediterranean coast beside Israel. The Philistines battled Israel for centuries, trying to take over their land. Israel had trouble fighting back because the Philistines were better organized and had better weapons. Only when David became king was Israel finally able to beat these bad guys.

Phoenicia (fo-*nee*-shee-a)

A long, narrow region along the Mediterranean coast to the north of Israel. The Phoenicians were famous as sailors, shipbuilders, and traders. Phoenicians aren't mentioned much in the Bible except for Hiram, David's friend. God later judged the Phoenician cities of Tyre and Sidon.

pierce

To poke a hole in something (or someone). Many people in Bible times pierced their ears, nose, and other body parts, just like people do today. A soldier pierced Jesus' side with a spear while he was on the cross to make sure Jesus was dead (John 19:34).

pig

An oinking animal known for rolling in the mud. Pigs are quite clean, but their smell can take your breath away. Pigs were one of the animals God told the Israelites not to eat. Their meat contained parasites that could make people sick (Leviticus 11:7).

pillar (*pil*-ler)

A tall wooden or stone post that helps to hold up a building. Many buildings in Bible times used pillars to support their roofs, such as the temple to Dagon that Samson destroyed (Judges 16:25–30). Pillars were also used as religious symbols and as property markers.

pillar of fire and cloud (*pil*-ler)

A miraculous sign God placed in the sky to lead the Israelites and remind them of his presence in the wilderness. God appeared in a pillar of cloud by day and a pillar of fire by night. Too bad God doesn't still lead us this way. It would be a lot easier than reading a map!

plague (plaig)

A display of God's power, sent as a punishment for sin and disobedience. Plagues usually took the form of disease or some other type of suffering. The best-known plagues are the ten plagues God sent on Egypt to convince Pharaoh to free the Israelites (Exodus 7:14–11:10; 12:29–30).

pleasing people

Giving in to peer pressure and following the crowd instead of God (Galatians 1:10). Peer pressure is tough to stand up to. When Moses led the Israelites in the wilderness, they constantly pressured him to do things their way instead of God's. But with God's help, he was able to stand firm.

plumb line (plum line)
A string with a weight on one end that was used to tell whether or not a wall is straight. Many prophets used the plumb line as an image to show that God was checking to see if Israel was straight or in line with God.

pomegranate (*pom*-e-gran-ate)
A round fruit about the size of an apple. Pomegranates have a tough skin that is filled with many delicious, red, pulp-covered seeds. Try one! Aaron's robe was decorated with images of pomegranates (Exodus 28:33–34). So was Solomon's temple (1 Kings 7:18, 20).

Pontius Pilate (*pon*-tee-us *pie*-let)
The Roman governor of Judah who sentenced Jesus to death. (What a horrible claim to fame.) Jesus' religious enemies would have killed Jesus themselves, but they needed permission from the Romans first. Pilate didn't want to give it to them, but he didn't want to make them mad. So he caved in to their demand.

Potiphar (*pot*-i-far)
The captain of Pharaoh's bodyguard who bought Joseph after he was sold into slavery. Potiphar was so impressed with Joseph that he put him in charge of his household. But when Potiphar's wife falsely accused Joseph of attacking her, Potiphar threw Joseph into prison.

praise (prayz)
To give someone approval or respect. We should praise everyone for the good things they do. But God deserves the *most* praise of all, because he's the reason we're all here! We can praise God in many ways, including prayer, singing, and by living godly lives.

prayer (*pray*-er)
Talking and listening to God. Prayer is how we thank God for what he has given us and ask him to become more involved in our lives. It's also a way of telling him what's on our hearts — what we feel, think, want, and need. It's like having a good conversation with someone you know and trust. And remember — you don't have to wait for a special occasion to pray. God is available to hear and answer your prayers twenty-four hours a day, seven days a week. So feel free to give him a call any time!

pregnant (*preg*-nunt)

When a woman has a baby growing in her womb, she's pregnant. Most pregnancies last about nine months. Women usually become pregnant through union with their husbands, but Mary, Jesus' mother, was made pregnant by the Holy Spirit (Luke 1:27–35). *That's* what you call a miracle!

Preparation Day (pre-par-*ay*-shun day)

The day before the Sabbath, the Passover, and other Jewish festivals. Preparation Day was a busy time. People cooked, cleaned, and took care of business so that they wouldn't have to work on the holy day, which began that day at sundown. Jesus was crucified on Preparation Day (John 19:14–42).

pretender (pree-*ten*-der)

Someone who says one thing then does another. Another name for a pretender is a hypocrite. Hypocrites aren't good, except at pretending (see Matthew 6). They're also good at pointing out the bad in others. Jesus spoke more harshly against hypocrites than any other group. Don't be a pretender!

pride

Thinking better of yourself than you should. Pride makes you think you are the center of the world and the king of the castle. It's an ugly sin that usually leads to more ugly sin (Proverbs 16:18). God wants us to be humble, not proud. That means putting others first.

priest (preest)

Someone who acted as a go-between for God and the people. When the people of Israel sinned, they brought a lamb, goat, or bull to the temple for the priest to sacrifice to God. We don't need a go-between today. We can ask God directly for forgiveness any time we need to!

Priscilla (pris-*sill*-ah)

The wife of Aquila. Priscilla and Aquila were forced to leave Rome when Emperor Claudius ordered all Jews out. Later they met with Paul and accompanied him from Corinth to Ephesus. There they met Apollos and taught him some of the finer points of the gospel.

prison (*priz*-un)

A place where criminals are locked up. In Bible times, caves and pits often served as prisons. Later prisons were built onto the king's palace. Sometimes good people were put in prison, such as Joseph, Peter, and Paul. God sent an angel to break Peter out of prison and an earthquake to break out Paul.

prisoners in Babylon (*pri*-zun-ers of *bab*-i-lawn)
God warned the people of Judah to change their lives, but they shut their ears. So God sent Nebuchadnezzar, king of Babylon, to attack them. Old Neb captured Jerusalem and hauled the Jews away to Babylon as prisoners, where they were forced to live for seventy years. This is called the Exile.

promise (*prah*-miss)
An agreement to do something, such as keep a secret, do a chore, or just plain be good. People don't always keep their promises, but God does. When the Bible says he'll do something, you can count on him to deliver the goods. So when *you* make a promise, be sure to keep it! See *oath*.

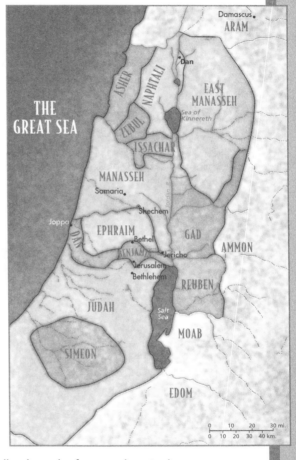

Promised Land (*prah*-missed land)
Canaan was the land God promised to Abraham and his descendants, the Israelites. The Promised Land was divided up among the twelve tribes of Israel. They lived there for centuries until the Romans booted them out after they revolted twice. The Jews finally returned two thousand years later.

prophecy (*praw*-feh-see)
Important words or messages — usually about the future — that God gives to his people. If people followed God, his promised blessings came. If people disobeyed God's warnings, the prophesied punishment hit them. (Can't say God didn't warn them!) The Old Testament contains many prophecies about Jesus.

prophet (*praw*-fet)
Someone who heard messages from God and told them to others. In the Old Testament, God sent several prophets to help his people stay on track. Famous prophets included Isaiah, Jeremiah, Ezekiel, and Daniel. The New Testament also mentions prophets such as Abagus and Philip's four daughters.

proverb (*prov*-erb)

A short saying that tells us something true about life. The book of Proverbs contains hundreds of these sayings. This book was written by wise men such as Solomon, who had learned a lot about God and life. Want to be wise? Take a look at this book.

psalm (sahm)

A poem, prayer, or song that praises God. David wrote dozens of psalms. These and others were collected into the book of Psalms, which was the Jewish hymnbook. Some psalms thank God for who he is. Others predict the future. And some simply ask for help.

Purim (*pure*-im)

A yearly feast to celebrate God delivering the Jews from death in Persia. Haman had convinced the king of Persia to kill every Jew in his empire, but Esther and Mordecai blew the lid on Haman's evil plans, and Haman wound up dead instead!

quail (kwale)

A bird similar to a grouse or a pheasant. Huge flocks of quail migrate every year to warmer climates, but these chubby little guys aren't made for long flights, and all that flying exhausts them. God used a bunch of exhausted quail to feed the Israelites in the wilderness (Exodus 16:13; Numbers 11:31–32).

queen (kween)

The wife of a king or the female ruler of a kingdom. The Bible mentions two good queens: the queen of Sheba, who came to learn from King Solomon, and Queen Esther, who saved the Jews in Persia. Unfortunately there were also *bad* queens like Jezebel and Athaliah.

queen of Sheba (kween of *she*-ba)

A queen from southern Arabia who thought the reports she was hearing about Solomon were too amazing to be true. She came to Jerusalem to see for herself and to test Solomon with all sorts of difficult questions. She discovered Solomon was even wiser and richer than she had heard!

R

rabbi (*rab*-eye)

A teacher of the Jewish law. Rabbi means "master" or "teacher." In Jesus' day, if you wanted to study the Scriptures, you had to find a rabbi to teach you. Once you did, you worked hard to learn from him and to live like him. That's how the disciples learned from their rabbi, Jesus.

raca (*rah*-ca)

Saying "raca" to someone was accusing the person of being a fool or evil. You may not say "raca," but it can be just as bad to accuse someone of being a fool, loser, *Dummkopf,* dipstick, doughhead, doofus, lamebrain, nerd, jerk, or idiot. Jesus forbade Christians to make accusations like that.

Rachel (*ray*-chul)

Jacob's second wife. Jacob slaved seven years as payment to marry Rachel. Problem was that Rachel's father Laban tricked Jacob by giving him her sister Leah instead. He then worked *another* seven years to pay for Rachel. Whew! Rachel wasn't able to have children for many years, but she finally had Joseph and Benjamin before she died. They became Jacob's favorite sons.

Rahab (*ray*-hab)

A woman from Jericho who hid two Israelites who were spying on the city. When soldiers came looking for the spies, Rahab sent them on a wild goose chase. Then she helped the spies escape out her window and away from the city. Rahab later became one of Jesus' ancestors.

rainbow (*rane*-bow)

A beautiful, multicolored bow that you can see arching across the sky if your back is to the sun while it is raining. Rainbows are caused by sunlight passing through raindrops in the air. They are God's way of assuring us that he will never again destroy the earth with a flood.

ransom (*ran*-some)

A payment demanded by kidnapers before they set someone free. The Bible says we've all been kidnapped by sin, and the ransom that sin demands is death. The good news is that Jesus paid our ransom by dying on the cross. If we believe in him, we can go free!

Rapture, the (*rap*-chur)
An event where every Christian is taken up into heaven. The Rapture will happen when Jesus returns to earth (1 Thessalonians 4:13–18). Every Christian who has died will return to life and rise up to meet him in the air. Then those who are still living will fly up into the sky too!

raven (*ray*-ven)
A large, black scavenger bird similar to a crow. Ravens will eat anything, even people's eyeballs (Proverbs 30:17). Jesus used ravens to show how God cares for us. He said that if God feeds the ravens, he won't let us go hungry. Thankfully, he won't ask us to eat the same thing!

Rebecca/Rebekah (ru-bek-uh)
Isaac's wife and the mother of Jacob and Esau. God chose Rebecca to be Isaac's wife, because she was hardworking and hospitable (Genesis 24). Rebecca was a good wife, but *wow*, did she ever pick favorites! When Isaac was near death, Rebecca helped Jacob steal Esau's birthright and blessing.

rebuke (re-*buke*)
To scold someone for something they've done wrong. For example, if your mom tells you to rake the lawn and you don't, she may rebuke you. Peter rebuked Jesus when Jesus said he was going to die, but Peter was *way* out of line. So Jesus rebuked him (Matthew 16:21–23).

redeemer (re-*deem*-er)
A person who sets someone free from slavery. Land that had been taken could also be redeemed. God describes himself as the Redeemer of Israel, because he freed them from slavery in Egypt (Isaiah 41:14). Jesus is our Redeemer because he set us free from sin (Mark 10:45).

Red Sea
The arm of sea between Egypt and the Sinai Peninsula. This is probably the sea God miraculously parted for the Israelites when they fled from Egypt. However, it's also possible that the Israelites crossed the "sea of reeds" just north of the Red Sea.

Rehoboam (re-ho-*bow*-um)
The son of Solomon and the last king of a united Israel. Rehoboam should have done well as king. But he blew it by listening to bad advice instead of the wisdom of his elders. As a result, the nation broke up and was never united again.

repentence   See *godly sadness*. (re-*pen*-tunce)

rest

A break from work or activity. This can mean a physical rest, like a nap or a vacation. It can also mean trusting God to take care of you and not worrying. Trust brings peace and rest. Yawn . . . think it's time for a nap.

resurrection (rez-zur-*rek*-shun)

Being brought back from the dead. After Jesus died on the cross, he lay in the tomb for three days. Then God raised him from the dead, proving that God is stronger than death. But that's not all. God promises that *every* Christian will one day be resurrected (Romans 6:5)!

revelation (rev-uh-*lay*-shun)

When God reveals something to his people through the Holy Spirit. In the Bible, God gave prophets and ordinary folks revelations through visions and dreams. The apostle John received a spectacular vision of the future. He described it all in the book of Revelation, the last book in the Bible.

revenge (re-*venge*)

Getting people back for something they've done to you. Revenge was a way of life during Old Testament times. That's where the saying "an eye for an eye" comes from (Exodus 21:23–25). But Jesus says revenge is God's business — not ours. We're supposed to love our enemies instead (Luke 6:27).

reward (re-*ward*)

A gift or prize you receive for doing something well. In heaven God will reward each one of us according to how we lived. But God doesn't just reward us after we die. If we obey him, we also receive rewards for our actions here on earth.

right hand

A place of honor, respect, and power. In Bible times, sitting at the right hand of the king or some other important person was the place to be. That meant you were their right-hand. Jesus sits at God's right hand (Romans 8:34).

Roman Empire (*ro*-mun *em*-pire)

The empire that controlled a large part of the world in Jesus' day. The Jews hated the Romans because they didn't like them messing in their affairs — or having to pay them taxes. But the Romans did many good things, such as providing good roads and keeping the peace.

Rome

The capital of the Roman Empire. Rome was a great city full of magnificent buildings, statues, and other works of art. Paul visited Rome on his missionary journeys. He probably also died there when Nero started persecuting Christians. The book of Romans was written to the church in Rome.

rule

Words that tell us the right way to do things. God has given us many rules for living. If you want to please God and have a great life, simply obey the rules God has given in the Bible. Your parents also give you rules. If you don't want to be grounded, you should obey those too!

Ruth

David's great-grandmother. When Ruth was a young woman, her husband and father-in-law died in Moab. So Ruth and her mother-in-law Naomi moved back to Bethlehem, Naomi's hometown. There Ruth married Boaz, who rescued her from a life of poverty. Ruth and Boaz became Jesus' ancestors.

S

Sabbath (*sab*-buth)
Sabbath means "rest." God made the world in six days, then rested on the seventh. That's why the Jews call Saturday the Sabbath. Some Christians still keep the Sabbath, but most Christians rest and worship God on Sunday, the day Jesus rose from the dead. See *Lord's Day.*

sacred (*say*-cred)
Set apart for God. Many things were considered sacred during Old Testament times. This included altars, food, priests' clothing, and anything used in sacrifices to God. In the Law, God gave the Israelites many rules for how sacred things were to be made and used. See *holy.*

sacrifice (*sa*-cru-fice)
To offer the life of something to God to receive forgiveness for sin. In Old Testament times, the Jews sacrificed animals, such as lambs, bulls, calves, goats, and doves, to God. The blood from these sacrifices covered their sin for a short time. Jesus came as the permanent sacrifice for sin.

Sadducees (*sad*-you-sees)
A religious group made up of the wealthy upper crust. Unlike the Pharisees, Sadducees didn't believe in angels or spirits or the resurrection of the dead. That's why they were "sad, you see." Sadducees felt that Jesus threatened their power and helped the Pharisees kill him.

saint
Someone set apart to do God's work. The Bible calls *every* Christian a saint (Romans 1:7). So the next time you're about to say, "I'm no saint," think again!

salt
A white, crystallized version of sodium chloride. Salt was used in Bible times to add flavor to food and prevent it from spoiling. Jesus called Christians the "salt of the earth" (Matthew 5:13), because we give the world flavor and help keep it from being spoiled by sin.

salvation (sal-*vay*-shun)
Deliverance from sin and its penalties. We are all born separated from God by sin. God's son Jesus is the only one who can offer us salvation. He died on the

cross to pay the penalty for our sins. Now we can be friends with God again. You can receive Jesus' salvation by becoming a Christian. All you have to do is admit that you've done wrong things and need forgiveness. Do that by telling God you're sorry and inviting Jesus to take control of your life. Congratulations, you've just received salvation!

Samaria (sa-*mare*-ee-uh)
1. The capital of the northern kingdom after the nation of Israel was divided. This was where Elijah and Elisha ministered. 2. In Jesus' day, Samaria was the entire land of the Samaritans, sandwiched between Judea on the south and Galilee on the north.

Samaritans (sah-*mare*-ih-tans)
After the Assyrians conquered the northern kingdom (Israel), they moved new people there. These foreigners married the remaining Israelites, and their descendants became the Samaritans. The Jews didn't like Samaritans, because they felt they weren't pure, and the Samaritans didn't worship God at the temple in Jerusalem.

Samson (*sam*-sun)
One of Israel's judges. Samson was so strong that he made Arnold Schwarzenegger seem like a featherweight. He once killed one thousand Philistines with a donkey's jawbone! The secret to Samson's strength was that his hair had never been cut. But Delilah found out his secret, snipped his locks, and let the Philistines capture him.

Samuel (*sam*-you-ul)
The last of the judges of Israel just before Israel had its first king. Samuel was a warrior and a prophet. He helped Israel defeat the Philistines, but he also brought them back to God. God also used Samuel to anoint Israel's first two kings — Saul and David.

Sanhedrin (san-*hee*-drin)
The Jewish high council in charge of religious matters and everyday life in Jesus' time. The seventy-one members of the Sanhedrin were made up of Pharisees, Sadducees, and one high priest. They even had their own police force to arrest people. It was the Sanhedrin who condemned Jesus to death.

Sapphira (saf-*fire*-rah)
A woman struck dead by God for trying to trick the church. Her husband Ananias had just keeled over after lying about the price he received for some property, when she walked in. Peter gave her a chance to tell the truth, but she didn't take it (Acts 5:7–11).

Sarah (sar-uh)

Abraham's wife. Sarah was incredibly beautiful even when she was more than seventy years old—so beautiful that Pharaoh was dying to marry her. Sarah couldn't have children. When God told her she'd have a baby in her old age, she burst out laughing. But God had the last laugh when Isaac was born.

Satan (say-tun)

An angel who led a rebellion against God and now works against God and the church. Satan is also called the devil, liar, Lucifer, Beelzebub, the Serpent, and the Dragon. You have to figure someone with that many ugly names would be a bad dude, and he is. Satan spends all of his time trying to distract people from following God. His number one trick is making evil look so good we'll want to take part in it. Don't be fooled. Jesus gave us the power to overcome Satan and his tricks (1 John 4:4).

Saul (sol)

The first king of Israel. Saul had everything the Israelites wanted in a king. He was tall, handsome, courageous, and humble. With God's help, Saul became a good king, and the people loved him. But later he disobeyed God so many times that he lost the job to David.

savior (sayv-your)

Someone who delivers others from evil or danger. This word is used to describe many people in the Bible, including the judges and some of Israel's kings. But it is mostly used to describe Jesus, who saved us from the greatest evil of all—sin.

scribe See teachers of the law.

Scripture (skrip-chur)

God's written Word. Scripture is another name for the Bible. Even though prophets, kings, apostles, fishermen, tax collectors, and other people wrote the Bible, all Scripture originally came from God (2 Timothy 3:16). God put the ideas in people's heads and then helped them write them down.

scroll

Sheets of papyrus or parchment sewn together and rolled onto sticks. Most of the Bible was originally written on scrolls. Scrolls that rolled and unrolled were the only books before books were invented. God told Ezekiel to eat a scroll (Ezekiel 3:3). Mmm ... yummy! Zechariah once saw a *flying* scroll (Zechariah 5:1).

seal

A ring with a pattern and/or words cut into it. It was pressed into wax or clay as a sort of signature. Seals were used to mark everything from scrolls to Jesus' tomb (Matthew 27:66). Revelation 9:4 talks about Christians receiving God's seal on their foreheads.

sea monster (see-*mon*-ster)

One of several words the Bible used to describe large sea creatures. They were also called serpents, great fish, whales, or Leviathan. No one knows exactly what these monsters were. They could have been gigantic eels, monster sharks, or some creature we have yet to discover.

Sea of Galilee (*gal*-i-lee)

A large, freshwater lake located about sixty miles north of Jerusalem. Peter, Andrew, James, and John were all fishermen on the Sea of Galilee before becoming Jesus' disciples. Jesus spent much of his time ministering near this lake. He even calmed a storm on it (Mark 4:35–41).

seer

Another name for a prophet (1 Samuel 9:9). A seer was literally someone who could *see* into the future (with God's help) or see into the heart of God. The seer then shared what he or she saw with those people God sent them to.

self-control

The strength to control your thoughts, words, and actions. Self-control is a fruit of the Spirit. Our sinful natures often make us want to do bad things. God gives us self-control so we can fight against those urges. Feeling tempted? Ask God to help you resist. He will!

selfish/selfishness (*sell*-fish/*sell*-fish-ness)

Putting your needs and wants before the needs and wants of others. People who are selfish are self-centered; they think the world revolves around them. But they're wrong. The world revolves around God — not us. That means we should always put him and others first. Otherwise we'll be out of the loop.

Sennacherib (sen-*ak*-er-rib)

An Assyrian king who decided to conquer Jerusalem but changed his mind after he woke up one morning and found most of his soldiers were dead (2 Kings 19:35). Sennacherib didn't wait around to find out what happened. He and his remaining soldiers headed home — pronto.

servant (*ser*-vunt)

A slave or a free person who worked for someone else, usually serving food, doing heavy labor, or running errands. Even though servants seem low on the totem pole, Jesus — who served us by giving his life for us — said those who serve are the greatest of all (Matthew 20:25–28).

Shadrach (*shad*-rack)

Daniel's friend who was thrown into a blazing furnace along with Meshach and Abednego because they wouldn't worship King Nebuchadnezzar's golden statue. All three of Daniel's friends went into the furnace and came out calm and cool. They didn't even smell like smoke.

sheep

Woolly animals used for food and clothing. Sheep are mentioned more often than *any* other animal in the Bible. They aren't very bright and need a shepherd to guide them. Jesus called us his sheep (John 10:27), because we also constantly need his help and guidance.

Shem

Noah's eldest son. Shem was blessed by Noah because he showed respect to his father (Genesis 9:20–27). That blessing came true in many ways for Shem when he became an ancestor of Jesus, the Messiah (Luke 3:36).

shepherd (*shep*-erd)

Someone who looks after sheep. Many of God's great leaders started as shepherds. Moses herded sheep for forty years. David was also a shepherd before he became king. God is called Israel's shepherd, because he guided them through every circumstance they encountered. Jesus also called himself "the good shepherd" (John 10:11).

shield (sheeld)

A round object usually made of wood, leather, and metal that protected soldiers in battle. Shields were usually strapped to a soldier's left arm. He used his right hand to attack with a sword or other weapon. Faith is also described as a shield (Ephesians 6:16).

ship

A vessel used to travel on the water. People who lived along the Mediterranean Sea used large ships for trade and war. The Phoenicians were known as the best shipbuilders. Although the Jews weren't much into sailing, Paul traveled by ship many times during his missionary journeys.

sickle (*sick*-ul)
A hand tool used to harvest grain. A sickle has a sharp, curved blade with a handle. Harvesters swing their sickles through the grain to cut it down. The grain is then gathered together into bundles called sheaves. Larger sickles are called scythes.

sickness (*sick*-nuss)
Poor health, usually caused by germs or viruses. It's no fun being sick, but God has given us many ways to get well. One way is to eat right, stay fit, and keep clean. Doctors can also help us with medicine. And God can heal us through prayer (James 5:14).

Sidon (*side*-en)
The most important Phoenician port city. Sidon was located on the coast of the Mediterranean and included several small islands connected by bridges. Sidon was attacked many times during its history but was rebuilt each time. It later became an important center for the early church.

siege (seej)
Surrounding a city or fortress to prevent supplies from going in and people from going out. This was a common war tactic used in Bible times. A siege could last for years, until the city's food and water supplies ran out. Then the people inside were forced either to give up or to starve.

Silas (*sigh*-las)
A man who joined Paul on his missionary journeys after Paul and Barnabas went their separate ways. In Philippi, Silas and Paul were beaten and thrown into jail. When they got out, they kept right on preaching. After Paul was martyred, Silas went to work with Peter.

Siloam, Pool of (sigh-*low*-am)
A water storage pond inside the walls of Jerusalem. Hezekiah's men dug a tunnel to a spring outside the city so there would be water if the city were besieged. Jesus healed a blind man by having him wash his eyes in this pool (John 9).

Simeon (New Testament) (*simmy*-un)
An old man who blessed Jesus in the temple. God promised Simeon he wouldn't die before he saw the Messiah. Sure enough, shortly after Jesus was born, Joseph and Mary walked in with their baby. Simeon prophesied over Jesus and nearly blew Mary and Joseph's socks — er, sandals — off.

S

Simeon (son of Jacob) (*simmy*-un)

Jacob's second son and father of one of the twelve tribes of Israel. Simeon is best known for helping Levi trick—then slaughter—all the men in Shechem, because the prince had attacked their sister Dinah. As a result, Jacob and his family had to pack up and split (Genesis 34).

Simon the Zealot (*sigh*-mun the *zel*-ut)

One of Jesus' twelve disciples. Simon was called the Zealot probably because he had once belonged to a radical group of Jews trying to overthrow the Romans. That's pretty much all we know about Simon.

sin

To disobey or displease God. The word *sin* literally means "to miss the mark." The first sin was when Adam and Eve disobeyed God. Now we all do it because their sin affected everyone. Sin can be anything—a thought, a word, or an action. The bad news is that sin separates us from God, and the penalty for sin is death. The good news is that Jesus died on the cross to pay the penalty for our sin. If we believe in Jesus, God forgives our sin, and we can have a relationship with him once again. Told you it was good news!

Sinai (*sigh*-nye)

A mountain in the Sinai Peninsula, also called Horeb. After the Israelites escaped from Egypt, God led them to Mount Sinai, where he put on a spectacular light show that included lightning, fire, and an earthquake. When it was all over, he gave them the Law and the Ten Commandments.

sinful nature See *flesh*. (*sin*-full *nay*-cher)

skills and abilities (skills and a-*bil*-i-tees)

Talents God gives us at birth. Our skills and abilities perfectly match who we are and what God wants us to do in life. Skills and abilities include things like singing, mathematics, and athletic ability. We should train and develop our skills and abilities and use them to help others.

slave

A person who is owned by someone else. When people were taken as prisoners of war during Bible times, they often became slaves. People who couldn't pay their debts were also sold into slavery. Jesus said that without God, we are all slaves to sin (John 8:34).

sling

A simple but deadly weapon made of a strip of leather with a pouch in the middle that holds a stone. A slinger swings the sling in a circle above his head and then lets go of one end of the leather to fire the stone. David killed Goliath with a sling.

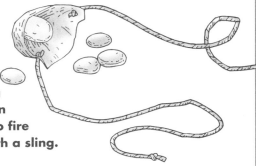

snake

A reptile with no legs. Snakes used to have legs, but they were forced to slither on their bellies after Satan disguised himself as a snake to tempt Eve (Genesis 3:14). God also gave Moses the power to turn his staff into a snake to convince Pharaoh to free the Israelites (Exodus 7:1–13).

Sodom and Gomorrah (sod-um and go-mor-ah)

Two cities south of the Dead Sea that were so wicked God had to destroy them. Abraham's nephew Lot was living in Sodom right before it was destroyed, but God's angels warned him to get out. Just in time too. Moments later, God rained down fire and obliterated the cities.

soldier (sole-jer)

A member of an army. Israel didn't have any soldiers at first. Instead, all Israelite men were trained how to use a particular weapon so they'd be able to fight when the need arose. But when Israel finally had a king, they built up an army just like other nations.

Solomon (sol-o-mun)

David's son and a great king who ruled over all of Israel. Solomon was the wisest man who ever lived. He received his wisdom as a special gift from God. Solomon built the temple in Jerusalem and wrote some of the Psalms and Proverbs as well as the Song of Songs and Ecclesiastes.

Son of Man

A name Jesus called himself to show that he was as much a man as he was God. Jesus was the Son of Man through his mother Mary and the Son of God through the Holy Spirit. He is humankind's representative to God *and* God's representative to humankind. Catch that?

soul (sole)

A person's entire life or being. We tend to think of our souls as only our inner selves or spirits. But the Jewish people used the word *soul* to describe their entire selves—body, mind, emotions, and spirit. To lose your soul is the same as losing your life (Mark 8:36–37).

spirit (*speer*-it)

The part of us that lives forever. Your spirit lives inside of your physical body. Without God, your spirit is dead because of sin. But Jesus and the Holy Spirit can make your spirit alive again. When your physical body dies, your spirit will go to live with God in heaven.

spiritual (*speer*-i-chul)

Of the spirit. Everyone is spiritual to some degree, because everyone has a spirit. But Christians are more spiritual than other people, because we have the Holy Spirit. That doesn't mean we're better than non-Christians. It just means we're more in tune with God. After all, he's right inside of us!

spiritual gifts See *gifts, spiritual.* (*speer*-i-chul)

spy

Someone who secretly gathers information about an enemy. Spies were often sent into enemy territory so that an army could know what they were up against before they went to war. For this reason, foreigners were often suspected of being spies. Israel sent spies into Canaan before they invaded.

staff

A stout stick used for walking or working. In Bible times, shepherds used staffs to guide their sheep or to fight off wild animals. Other people used them as walking sticks or crutches. Kings also used short staffs (scepters) as signs of their authority.

standing firm (*stand*-ing ferm)

The ability to stay strong even when everything is pulling us the wrong way. This is also called perseverance. Jesus promises to give you the strength to do this (Philippians 3:13–14). Each time you stand firm, he makes you even stronger. All you need to do is keep your eyes on him.

star

A giant ball of hot, burning gas in outer space. Stars are mentioned often in the Bible. God promised Abraham that he would have as many descendants as there are stars. That's a lot of grandkids! God also announced the birth of Jesus with a special star (Matthew 2:1–11).

stealing (*steel*-ing)

Taking something without permission when it doesn't belong to you. Stealing is on God's top ten list of don'ts (Exodus 20:15). It's a sin because it shows you don't trust God to provide for you and you think your needs are more important than the needs of others.

Stephen (*stee*-fen)

A leader in the early church who was the first Christian to be martyred. Stephen was a powerful preacher who also did many miracles. The religious leaders didn't like what Stephen was doing, so they dragged him outside the city and stoned him (Acts 7:54–60).

stoning (*stone*-ing)

The main form of execution used by the Israelites. To stone someone meant to throw stones (rocks) at a person until he or she died. The witnesses to the crime had to throw the first stones. Stephen, the first martyr, was stoned. So was Paul, but he didn't die (Acts 14:19–20).

story (*store*-ee)

Jesus told many stories to help people understand God. These stories were called parables. Each parable contained a lesson about God. Famous parables include the story of the lost son (Luke 15:11–32) and the story of the foolish virgins (Matthew 25:1–13). Old Testament prophets also told parables.

stubborn/stubbornness
(*stub*-born/*stub*-born-ness)

Unwillingness to change or give in. Refusing to budge an inch can be good when we don't give in to sin. But self-willed stubbornness stops us from growing closer to God and others — or makes us refuse to stop sinning. Dig your feet in, yes, but for the right reasons!

suffering (*suf*-fer-ing)

Physical, mental, or emotional pain. Suffering is part of the Curse, and people have suffered ever since Adam and Eve sinned. Suffering is never fun, but God can use it to make us stronger. Remember that the next time you're going through a difficult time.

sun

The closest star to earth. The sun makes life possible by providing light and heat. Many people in Bible times worshiped the sun, but God proved he was greater than the sun by holding it still for Joshua (Joshua 10:13) and moving it backward for Hezekiah (Isaiah 38:8).

sword (sord)

A weapon used for stabbing or slashing. Hebrew swords were usually quite short — between eighteen and twenty-four inches long. They had a straight blade that was sharpened on both sides. It was the basic weapon of most warriors. God's Word is called the "sword of the Holy Spirit" (Ephesians 6:17).

synagogue (sin-ah-gog)

A building where Jews gather to worship God, read the Scriptures, and pray. Once the Jews did these things only in the temple, but after the Babylonians destroyed it, the Jews built synagogues instead. Every town had its own synagogue. Jesus and the apostles often taught in synagogues.

Syria See *Aram.* (seer-ee-ah)

T

tabernacle See *holy tent.* (tab-er-nak-ul)

talent See *skills and abilities.* (tal-unt)

talking back (tok-ing back)

Mouthing off to your parents when they ask you to do something. It's important not to talk back to those in authority (Titus 2:9). You should respect your elders, whether they're your parents or not (1 Timothy 5:1). Being old is difficult enough without receiving disrespect.

tambourine (tam-ber-een)

A hand-held drum made of skin stretched over a wooden hoop. No one knows if tambourines had metal cymbals on them like modern tambourines, but tambourines were a popular instrument in Bible times.

tassels (tass-els)

Bunches of thread that Israelites sewed onto the corners of their clothing for decorations. God told them to do this as a reminder to keep his commandments (Deuteronomy 22:12). Cool! How's *that* for a fashion statement? The tassels also had a blue cord (Numbers 15:38–39).

taxes (*tax*-ez)

Money paid to the government. The government then provides protection and services for the community or nation. People in Judea paid taxes on everything they bought and sold. Another tax went to pay for the temple. Jesus told Peter he would find the money to pay their taxes in the mouth of a fish — and he did (Matthew 17:24–27)!

tax collector (tax col-*lect*-or)

Men who collected taxes from the Jews to give to the Romans. The Jews hated tax collectors because they always took more than they were supposed to and kept the extra for themselves. Jesus chose Matthew, a tax collector, as his disciple. Zacchaeus was also a tax collector (Luke 19:1–10).

teachers of the law (*tee*-chers)

Expert writers (scribes) who made copies of the Scriptures. Think of them as human photocopiers with photographic memories. Many scribes wrote out the Scriptures so many times that they memorized huge chunks of them. That's how they became respected teachers of the law.

teachings (*tee*-chings)

A group of beliefs about God, Jesus, humanity, and the church, also called doctrines. Teachings are important truths central to the Christian faith, such as, "There is one God" and "Jesus is God's Son." The main doctrine of Christians is summed up in the Apostles' Creed.

temple (*tem*-pull)

A magnificent place of worship. Solomon built a colossal temple to God in Jerusalem. It lasted for nearly five hundred years, until the Babylonians destroyed it. The temple was rebuilt, but it was not nearly as impressive. Centuries later, Herod rebuilt the temple again. That was the temple Jesus went to.

temptation (tem-*tay*-shun)

A desire to do something wrong. Being tempted isn't wrong, but giving in to temptation is. Satan tempted Jesus in the desert, but Jesus didn't sin (Luke 4:1–13). In fact, he *never* sinned! God can help you resist temptation too. Just ask him.

Ten Commandments, the (ten co-*mand*-munts)

God's basic guidelines for living. God engraved them into stone tablets and gave them to Moses and the Israelites on Mount Sinai. The Ten Commandments were part of a covenant God made with the Israelites in which they agreed to be his people and he agreed to be their God. These commandments are still important today, because they show us who God is and how we should live. They cover things like how to worship God, how to treat other people's property, and how to treat our parents. Important stuff! You can take a look at them in Exodus 20.

tenth
In Old Testament times, God commanded the Israelites to give the first tenth of their crops and animals to the priests. This was called a tithe. Tithing showed that the Israelites trusted God and were thankful for his care. Many Christians still tithe for the same reasons today.

Tent of Meeting See *holy tent.*

test
A way of finding out how strong someone is. God tests us to help us grow and make us more like Jesus. Testing can be difficult, but it's usually worth it in the end. Just think — when you get to heaven, you'll get to read your report card!

testament (*test*-uh-ment)
Another word for "covenant" or "will." The first covenant between God and humankind was the Law of Moses. The story of how God gave this testament is told in the Old Testament. The second testament — talked about in the New Testament — went into effect when Jesus died on the cross.

thankfulness (*thank*-full-ness)
An attitude of appreciation toward God and others for the things they do for you. God is so wonderful and loving that there's no end to the list of things to thank him for — life, health, friends, family, wisdom, food, money, clothing, you name it! Having trouble being thankful? Just open your eyes!

Thessalonica (thess-a-loan-eye-ca)
The most important seaport in Macedonia (northern Greece). Paul visited Thessalonica on his second missionary journey, and (as often happened) he got himself into trouble for preaching the gospel (Acts 17:1–9). First and Second Thessalonians were written to the church in Thessalonica.

thief (theef)
Someone who steals. The Law had strict rules for dealing with thieves. Thievery was also a serious crime in Jesus' day. Jesus was crucified between two thieves, one of whom became a Christian. Jesus also said he would return one day like a thief in the night (Luke 12:35–40).

Thomas (*taw*-muss)

One of Jesus' twelve disciples. Thomas is best known for doubting that Jesus had really risen from the dead. He thought the rest of the disciples were seeing things. Thomas said he wouldn't believe unless he poked his finger into the nail holes in Jesus' hands. He soon got that chance.

threshing floor
(*thresh*-ing flore)

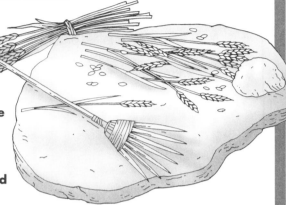

A hard, smooth, flat surface on which people pounded sheaves of grain until the seeds fell out. The seeds were then gathered up and ground into flour. Tops of rocks often made good threshing floors. Ruth met her husband Boaz on a threshing floor.

throne

A fancy seat that only the king is allowed to sit on — much better than your dad's favorite armchair. God promised King David that one of his descendants would always sit on the throne of Israel. This was fulfilled through Jesus, who sits enthroned in heaven.

Tiberius Caesar (tie-*beer*-ee-us *see*-zur)

The second emperor of Rome. Tiberius was the Caesar the Pharisees referred to when they tried to trick Jesus into saying they shouldn't pay taxes to Caesar (Matthew 22:15–22). Jesus said Caesar could have the money due to him but our praise should go to God.

Timothy (*tim*-uh-thee)

A young man who became one of Paul's closest friends and helpers. During his missionary journeys, Paul trained Timothy to preach the gospel and strengthen believers. Timothy was eventually put in charge of the church in Ephesus. The letters 1 and 2 Timothy were written by Paul to encourage him.

tithe See *tenth*.

Titus (*tie*-tus)

A Gentile believer who helped Paul on his missionary journeys. Titus isn't mentioned in the book of Acts, but Paul talks about him in several letters, including Galatians and 2 Corinthians. The Bible also contains a letter that Paul wrote to Titus, which explains the qualities required for church leaders.

tomb (toom)

A place where dead bodies were placed. Tombs were often located inside caves with a large stone blocking the doorway to keep out animals and grave robbers. When Jesus died, his body was placed in a tomb. But he didn't stay there for long. On the third day, he rose again!

tongue (tung)

The organ we use for talking and tasting. We should always use our tongues to help and encourage people, not to hurt them. You'd never know it, but that little wagging thing in your mouth can be quite dangerous (James 3:5–6). In the Bible, tongue also means "language."

tower (tow-er)

A tall building built to defend a city and allow watchmen to see a long distance in all directions. Towers were often built at the corners of city walls and on either side of the city gates. Farmers built small towers in their fields to guard against thieves.

tradition (tra-dish-un)

Beliefs, customs, and practices passed from one generation to the next. Traditions can be good things, because they help us remember and honor the past. But sometimes, human customs get in the way of what God wants. They did for the Pharisees (Matthew 15:2).

training (train-ing)

Instruction, correction, and discipline designed to help you learn. Training means practicing certain skills so you're able to use them when the need arises. When God and your parents instruct, correct, and discipline you, think of them as coaches who are helping you prepare for the big game — life.

translation (trans-lay-shun)

Saying one language's words in a different language. Believe it or not, the Bible wasn't originally written in English. For you to read the Bible, scholars had to translate it from Hebrew, Greek, and Aramaic, the original Bible languages. The Bible has been translated into nearly three hundred languages!

treaty (tree-tee)

An agreement between two nations. Treaties were made for trade agreements or military alliances. During Bible times, smaller nations often made treaties when they needed help to fight a larger enemy. Israel eventually got in trouble when it started relying on treaties instead of God.

tribes, twelve

The descendants of the twelve sons of Jacob (Israel). Each of Jacob's sons had a family, and while the Israelites were in Egypt, these families became *very* large and were called tribes. When they conquered Canaan, every tribe received a piece of land — except the Levites, who were the priests.

Tribulation, the (trib-u-*lay*-shun)

A time of great suffering at the end of time. It will include wars, natural disasters, and all sorts of strange and terrible events all over the earth. The Tribulation is predicted in the book of Daniel (Daniel 7–12) and is mentioned in Revelation 7:14.

Trinity (*trin*-i-tee)

The doctrine that teaches that there is only one God and he exists as three equal persons — Father, Son, and Holy Spirit. You can see the Trinity at Jesus' baptism (Matthew 3:16–17). Jesus the Son was in the water, the Holy Spirit came down like a dove, and God the Father spoke from heaven. This shows that God isn't Jesus one day, the Holy Spirit the next, and God the Father the day after that. He is all three persons at once all of the time! Hard to understand? Yes, but it just shows how great God is compared with our puny brains.

Troas (*tro*-as)

An important city on the coast of Asia Minor. Paul visited Troas many times on his missionary journeys. One night he preached so long that a young man dozed off and tumbled out of a third-story window (Acts 20:5–12). Hopefully, your pastor doesn't have that effect on you!

trumpet (*trum*-pet)

An instrument made from a ram's or a goat's horn. Trumpets could also be made of bone or metal. Hebrew trumpets weren't much like the ones we have today. They had no keys and were only about two feet long. Trumpets were used in worship and to rally troops in battle.

trust

A belief in the goodness, fairness, and love of a person. Without trust, relationships can't exist. A person can never be sure that the other person will hold up his or her end of the bargain. You can completely trust God, though. He will never let you down (Psalm 9:10).

trustworthy (*trust*-werth-ee)

Deserving or *worthy* of trust. Someone who is trustworthy will always act with your best interest in mind. God is completely trustworthy. He is *able* to do more than we could ever ask or imagine (Ephesians 3:20–21) *and* we can count on him to always come through.

truth *(trooth)*

Anything that lines up with God, his character, and his Word (the Bible). Jesus said he is the way, the truth, and the life (John 14:6) and promised that the Holy Spirit will guide us into all truth (John 16:13). Anything that is not true does not come from God.

truthful *(trooth-*full)*

Full of truth. Someone who is truthful is reliable and honest and won't tell a lie. We should always be truthful, because God is truth. Telling the truth can be difficult, especially when it gets you into trouble, but God never said being truthful would be easy — just *right.*

tunic *(too-*nik)*

A light shirt worn under a person's outer clothing. Tunics covered only down to the hips or knees, and if that's all someone was wearing, he was considered to be naked. That's all David wore when he danced before God (2 Samuel 6:20), and all Peter wore when he was fishing (John 21:7).

Tyre *(tie-*er)*

An important Phoenician seaport and a sister city to Sidon. The Tyrians were mostly on good terms with Israel. They provided supplies for David's palace and Solomon's temple. Tyre began as a coastal city, but when Nebuchadnezzar came to attack them, they packed up their city and moved to an offshore island.

U

unclean *(un-*cleen)*

Impure or unfit. In Old Testament times, God labeled foods, animals, and other items as either clean or unclean. Clean items could be used by the Israelites. Unclean items could not. God did this to teach the Israelites how to be holy, just like him (Leviticus 11:44).

unicorn (*you*-ni-corn)
A mythical creature like a horse but with a long, spiral horn on its forehead. In older Bible versions, the Hebrew word *reem* used to be translated "unicorn." But most scholars today think these *reem* refers to the auroch, a wild ox that is now extinct (see Numbers 23:22).

Urim and Thummim (*yer*-im and *thum*-mim)
Gems that the high priest used to make important decisions. The Urim and Thummim were worn inside the high priest's breastplate. Some scholars think they were rolled like dice or glowed to show yes or no. However, it's likely God simply spoke to the priest when he wore the breastplate.

unleavened bread (un-*lev*-end bred)
Flat bread made without yeast (leaven). God told the Israelites to eat unleavened bread along with the Passover lamb the night God's angel killed all the firstborn sons in Egypt. This tradition is continued every year at Passover.

Unleavened Bread, Feast of
See *Passover.* (un-*lev*-end bred)

Ur (er)
Abraham's hometown. Ur was located in Mesopotamia on the banks of the Euphrates River. It was a large, prosperous city. The people of Ur worshiped many false gods. Their chief god (the moon) was named Sin, of all things. They worshiped him on pyramid-towers called ziggurats.

Uriah (*yer-ri*-uh)
A Hittite soldier and Bathsheba's first husband. When Uriah was off at war, David committed adultery and got Bathsheba pregnant. David tried to cover up his crime, but when that didn't work, he had Joab assign Uriah to a spot in the battle where he would be killed. And he was.

Uzziah (u-*zi*-uh)
Ninth king of Judah and father of Jotham. Uzziah became king at age sixteen and ruled for a whopping fifty-two years. He did a good job for the most part. Later in life, Uzziah insisted on doing a job only the priests could do. God punished Uzziah by giving him leprosy.

V

Vashti (*vash*-tee)

Wife of Xerxes, king of Persia. One night, Xerxes wanted to show off Vashti's beauty to his guests. When Vashti refused, Xerxes banished her from the palace and chose Esther as queen in her place. Good thing, too, because that allowed Esther to save the Jews.

veil (vale)

1. A woman's head covering. Moses also wore a veil to hide his face after meeting with God (Exodus 34:33). 2. A curtain that separated the Holy Place from the Most Holy Place in the tabernacle and later in the temple. When Jesus died, this veil was torn in two (Matthew 27:51).

vengeance See *revenge.* (*ven*-juns)

vine

A plant (like a grapevine) that creeps along the ground or climbs up things. Jesus said he is the true vine, and we are all branches. If we stay connected to Jesus, we'll bear lots of fruit—just like branches that stay on the vine.

vineyard (*vin*-yard)

A place where grapes are grown. Vineyards during Bible times were always fenced and had a tower to keep out animals and thieves. They also contained a winepress so that grapes could be harvested and juiced. Jesus mentioned vineyards in many of his parables.

virgin (ver-jin)

A person who has never had sexual intercourse. Mary, the mother of Jesus, was a virgin, but by a miracle of the Holy Spirit, she became pregnant with Jesus. Isaiah prophesied this miracle hundreds of years earlier (Isaiah 7:14).

vision (*viz*-un)

A dreamlike picture that God gave people while they were awake — not asleep. A vision usually had all sorts of strange images and words and gave the person who received it insights about God. God spoke through visions to many prophets, including Ezekiel, Daniel, and the apostle John.

W

wafer (*way*-fur)

A thin cracker made of unleavened flour. Wafers were used in offerings to God, as when Aaron and his son became priests or when people became Nazirites (Numbers 6:7). Wafers were made without yeast to symbolize how we should be without sin. Remember that next time you eat a cracker!

wages (*way*-jus)

The payment someone receives for work. The Bible uses wages to describe the payment we receive for sin (Romans 6:23). What is *that* payment? Death. You can't cash that at the bank! Instead of making us richer, sin only makes us poorer. Better to work for God instead.

war (wor)

A battle between two armies. The Israelites fought wars throughout much of their history. They had to fight to conquer the Promised Land and then to hold on to it. God often helped the Israelites in strange, miraculous ways — like how he helped Joshua defeat the Amalekites (Exodus 17:8–16).

water (*wah*-ter)

A clear liquid necessary for life. Clean water was pretty rare in Bible lands. After the rainy season ended, the water quickly drained away. Jesus promised to give us living water (John 4:13–14). Drink it, and you'll never be thirsty again! Small wonder water became a symbol of life.

weapon (*weh*-pun)

A tool used to fight in battle. In Bible times, most people used roughly the same types of weapons. These included swords, daggers, bows and arrows, slings, spears, and clubs for fighting. Then there were shields and other armor for defense. Weapons were first made of wood and stone, then bronze, then iron.

wedding (*wed*-ing)

The ceremony that joins a man and woman in marriage. Weddings were joyous events in Bible times. Everyone got involved. The biggest, most wonderful wedding of all will take place when we get to heaven and are joined with Jesus forever (Revelation 19:7–9). If you're a Christian, you'll be part of the wedding party!

weed

An unwanted plant. A common weed in Israel was the tare. Farmers usually let the tares grow quite large (so they could tell the difference between them and wheat) before they pulled them up by the roots. Jesus compared wicked people with tares in Matthew 13:24–30.

well

A deep hole in the ground that provides water. Wells in Bible times were very important because water was so scarce during the summer months. People even fought for ownership of the wells! Wells were often located just outside of town and were key meeting places for the community.

widow (*wid*-oh)

A woman whose husband has died. In Bible times, when a woman lost her husband, it often meant big trouble. Women had few ways to provide for themselves and their children. God made laws to help widows survive (e.g., Deuteronomy 26:12). We should also help widows (James 1:27).

will

The part of us that makes decisions. One of the greatest gifts God has given us is a will. The Holy Spirit draws us to God, but we *choose* either to love and serve God or to sin. We should love God so that we want *his* will to be done, not ours (Matthew 6:10).

wind

The movement of air as a result of the weather. Israel had four main winds: a cold, dry wind from the north; a hot, fierce wind from the east; a moist wind from the west; and a soft wind from the south. Jesus compared the Holy Spirit with the wind (John 3:8).

wine

An alcoholic drink made from fermented grapes. Wine was a common drink during Bible times. It was even used in worship and as medicine. Although Jesus' first miracle was turning water into wine (John 2:1–11), Paul reminded us that believers should be filled with the Holy Spirit, not booze (Ephesians 5:18).

winepress (*wine*-press)

A place where grapes are pressed (crushed) to make wine. Winepresses were usually carved into a large rock in the vineyard so the grapes could be squashed as they were harvested. In the end times, Jesus will crush his enemies like grapes in a winepress (Revelation 19:11–15). Youch!

wineskin (*wine*-skin)

A container made from goatskin and used for holding wine. New wine could not be put in old, stiff wineskins because the fermentation process would cause them to burst. Jesus used this process to explain how the old wineskin of the law could not contain the "new wine" of grace (Luke 5:36–37).

wisdom (*wiz*-dum)

The ability to make fair judgments and tell the difference between right and wrong. Wisdom comes from God. We cannot have wisdom until we learn to love and respect God and others (Proverbs 9:10). The Bible says wisdom is more valuable than gold or treasure. That makes sense. Money can only buy you stuff, but wisdom can help you live a long, prosperous life that pleases God and others — and *that's* priceless. A good place to learn about wisdom is in Proverbs, because most of the proverbs were written by Solomon, the wisest man who ever lived.

wise men

Scholars from Iraq or Persia who studied the stars. The wise men saw a star that indicated that the king of the Jews had been born. They followed it to Bethlehem, where they found Jesus. There were possibly three wise men, but there could have been more. We don't know the exact number for sure.

witchcraft (*witch*-craft)

The practice of magic, sorcery, and other occult activities. This includes things like casting spells, predicting the future, controlling evil spirits, or contacting the dead. God strictly forbids the practice of witchcraft (Deuteronomy 18:10–12). God does not like witchcraft because it is evil and distracts people from following him.

witness (*wit*-nuss)

In ancient Israel, witnesses were people who had seen a crime and then told a judge about it. A witness could also tell others about a good thing. We can be witnesses for Jesus by telling others what he has done in our lives.

worship (*wer*-ship)

To give praise, honor, glory, and respect to God. Only God deserves our worship, because he created everything. Worshiping anything or anyone else would be just plain *dumb*. It only leads to trouble. We can worship God anytime and anywhere by singing, praying, and obeying his Word.

Word, the

1. The Word of God, the Bible. 2. The English translation of the Greek word *logos*. John used this word to describe how Jesus made God fully known to humankind by coming to earth as a man (John 1:1–14). Before Jesus, we had a dim idea of God. Jesus came to turn on the lights.

work

Physical or mental activity. God didn't create us just to sit around like slugs and watch TV. He created us to work, just as he works. Paul said that if a person doesn't work, he or she shouldn't eat. But work isn't all there is to life, so make sure you take time to relax too.

world (werld)

1. Everything God has created, including the earth, the sun, the stars, and outer space. 2. The corrupt systems of people. "World" is often used to describe the world of sinful people who oppose the things of God. People who focus on this world instead of God are called worldly.

wrath of God, the (rath of God)

God's righteous anger over sin. God loves us and wants to be with us, but sin keeps us apart. Nothing sinful can enter his holy presence. That's why God gets upset about sin. He wants us to be with him, but we can't. Jesus came to fix this problem.

X

Xerxes (zerks-zees)

The king of Persia from 486–465 B.C. Xerxes had some problems with his wife Vashti, so he sent her away and made Esther the queen instead. God used Esther's position as queen to save the Jews from being killed by Haman.

Y

Yahweh (yaw-way)

A name for God that means "I am who I am." We don't really know if Yahweh is the proper pronunciation of this word, because the Jews considered God's name to be so holy that they wrote only the consonants, not the vowels. God gave himself this name when he first appeared to Moses (Exodus 3:14).

Year of Jubilee (yeer of ju-bi-lee)

A special year of rest and rejoicing that was supposed to take place every fifty years in Israel. No crops could be planted, any money owed was forgiven, slaves were set free, and property went back to its first owner. Unfortunately, the Israelites never did stick to this plan (Jeremiah 34:8–17).

yeast (yeest)

A sour, fermented substance added to dough to make it rise. Another word for yeast is *leaven*. Every year the Hebrews celebrated the Feast of Unleavened Bread. The Bible warns that hatred and sin is like yeast. A little bit will quickly spread (1 Corinthians 5:6–7).

yoke
A wooden bar placed over the necks of two oxen so they could pull a cart or plow. The yoke was also used in the Bible to represent a burden. Jesus promises that if we take his yoke upon ourselves, life will go much better for us because his yoke is light (Matthew 11:29–30).

Z

Zacchaeus (za-*kee*-us)
A tree-climbing, tax-collecting bona fide short guy from Jericho whose life was changed when Jesus came to visit. Zacchaeus was so overwhelmed by Jesus' love that he gave half his money to the poor and repaid everyone he had stolen from. Jesus visited Zacchaeus to show he had come to save sinners.

Zadok (*zay*-dok)
A high priest and true friend during David's reign. He was one of the only people to remain faithful to David until the end. When Absalom rebelled against David, Zadok stuck with him. And when David was dying, Zadok helped expose a plot and made sure Solomon became king.

Zarephath (*zair*-e-fath)
A city on the coast of Phoenicia. The prophet Elijah stayed in Zarephath with a widow and her son during a great famine. All she had was a handful of flour and some oil, but God rewarded her hospitality by miraculously refilling her flour bin and oil jug each day.

Zealots (*zel*-lots)
A radical Jewish religious group that fought against the Romans. The Zealots were like guerrillas. They attacked and killed the Romans and those who cooperated with them. The Zealots led a revolt and were eventually defeated by the Romans. Simon, one of Jesus' disciples, was a Zealot before he met Jesus.

Zebedee (*zeb*-e-dee)
The father of James and John, two of Jesus' twelve disciples. Zebedee's sons literally left him holding the net when Jesus came by. One word from Jesus, and they were out of there. Zebedee probably wasn't too keen about losing his help, but his wife was all for it!

Zebulun (*zeb*-u-lun)

Jacob's tenth son and father of one of the twelve tribes of Israel. Zebulun's tribe played an important part in the battles of the judges. But beyond that, either Zebulun didn't do much or people forgot to write it down, because we know almost nothing more about him. Nada. Zip.

Zechariah (prophet) (zek-ar-eye-ah)

A prophet who helped rebuild the temple after the Jews returned from captivity in Babylon. He worked alongside Ezra and the prophet Haggai to lead the people. Zechariah's prophecies zero in on the coming of the Messiah. You can read them in the book of — you guessed it — Zechariah.

Zechariah (New Testament) (zek-ar-*eye*-ah)

Father of John the Baptist. When Zechariah was an old man, an angel told Zechariah that he and his wife Elizabeth would have a son. The angel said to name him John. Zechariah had trouble believing it, so God didn't allow him to speak until his son was born.

Zedekiah (zed-e-*ky*-ah)

The last king of Judah. He was a puppet ruler installed by Nebuchadnezzar to keep Judea in line. Jeremiah warned Zedekiah to behave, but after several years, puppet Zed broke his strings and rebelled. Nebuchadnezzar then attacked Jerusalem, captured Zedekiah, and put out his eyes.

Zephaniah (zef-an-*eye*-ah)

A prophet to Judah right before the Jews were carried off to Babylon. Zephaniah predicted that God would judge Judah, but he would save a few people who would continue to serve him. His prophecies are in the book of Zephaniah.

Zerubbabel (zare-*roo*-ba-bell)

Leader of the Jews sent to Jerusalem by Cyrus the Great to rebuild the temple. Construction went well for the first two years, but conflicts with the Samaritans delayed things for seventeen years. Zerubbabel finally got back to work, and the temple was completed four years later.

ziggurat (*zig*-ger-ot)
A tall temple shaped something like a pyramid only with steps all the way

up. Ziggurats were built by the Babylonians, Sumerians, and Assyrians to help them get closer to their gods, who supposedly lived in the sky. The tower of Babel (Genesis 11:4) was a type of ziggurat.

Zion (zy-on)
The hill upon which the city of Jerusalem stood. The name Zion was later used for the entire city of Jerusalem, which spread out beyond that hilltop. In the New Testament, Zion stands for God's heavenly kingdom, the New Jerusalem (Hebrews 12:22).

Zipporah (zip-por-ah)
Moses' wife. Zipporah is known for being pretty quick with a knife. God was going to kill Moses because he didn't circumcise his son Eliezer. But Zipporah grabbed Eliezar and a stone knife and quickly did the job. Eliezer probably wasn't too happy about it, but Moses lived to tell the tale.

The first NIrV reference library for kids!

Kidatlas

Important Places in the Bible and Where to Find Them

Written by Rick Osborne, Ruth van der Maas, and Marnie Wooding

Hardcover 0-310-70059-0

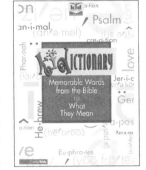

Kidictionary

Memorable Words from the Bible and What They Mean

Written by Rick Osborne and Kevin Miller

Hardcover 0-310-70077-9

Kidcordance

Big Ideas from the Bible and Where to Find Them

Written by Rick Osborne with Ed Strauss and Kevin Miller

Hardcover 0-310-22472-1

Halley's Bible Kidnotes

Bite-sized Bible Facts and Where to Find Them

Written by Dr. Henry H. Halley with Jean Syswerda

Hardcover 0-310-70117-1

Zonder**kidz**™

Grand Rapids, MI 49530
www.zonderkidz.com

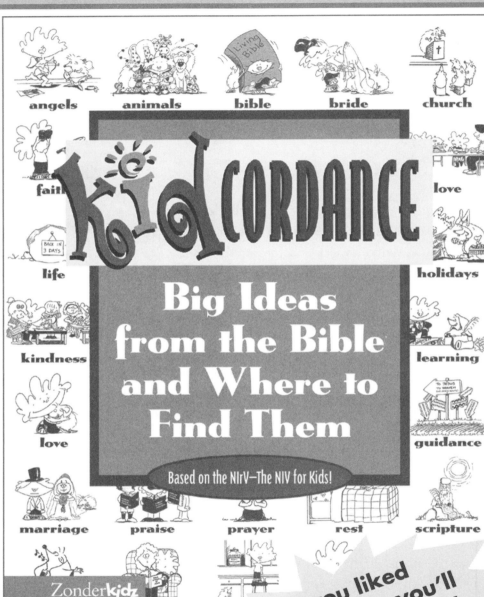

angels animals bible bride church

faith love

life holidays

KidCORDANCE

Big Ideas from the Bible and Where to Find Them

Based on the NIrV—The NIV for Kids!

kindness learning

love guidance

marriage praise prayer rest scripture

Zonderkidz

song study

If you liked Kidictionary, you'll love Kidcordance!

Aaron

Aaron was Moses' older brother. We first read about him when God called him to help Moses convince Pharaoh to set the Israelites free from slavery. God used Aaron to speak for Moses because Moses couldn't speak well, and Aaron was a good speaker. Later, God made Aaron, his sons, and their descendants the priests of Israel.

HE LOVES FROGS, AND HE JUST READ HOW AARON HELD HIS ROD OVER THE PONDS OF EGYPT AND FROGS CAME UP AND COVERED THE LAND.

EGYPT— Plague of frogs Welcome!

Key Verse

"Aaron told them everything the Lord had said to Moses. He also did the miracles in the sight of the people." (Exodus 4:30)

What about your brother, Aaron the Levite?
Later on, Moses and Aaron went to Pharaoh. They said ...
They said ... "Come. Make us a god that will lead us."
He must be appointed by God, just as Aaron was.

Exodus 4:14
Exodus 5:1–6:12
Exodus 32:1–35
Hebrews 5:1–4

Abba

In Aramaic (the language Jesus spoke) Abba means "Daddy" or "Papa." In Jesus' time, "Abba" was what children called their father. Jesus used this word when he prayed to God in the Garden of Gethsemane. He called God "Abba," or "Daddy," to show his disciples that God loves us like a father loves his children.

Key Verse

"You received the Holy Spirit, who makes you God's child. By the Spirit's power we call God *'Abba.' Abba* means Father." (Romans 8:15)

How much more will your Father ... give good gifts to ...
Abba means Father.
He gave them the right to become children of God.
By his power we call God "*Abba*."

Matthew 7:11
Mark 14:36
John 1:12–13
Galatians 4:6

Abraham

Abraham lived in the city of Ur. One day God told him to move to Canaan. So Abraham left with his wife, Sarah, and their belongings. God made an agreement (a "covenant") with Abraham. He promised that Abraham would have as many descendants as there are stars. That sounded strange, because Abraham had no children, and he was 100 years old and Sarah was 90! God also promised that Abraham would become a blessing to the world. God kept his promises! Abraham had a son, Isaac, and Isaac's

family grew into a nation—the Jews. And through his most important descendant, Jesus, Abraham has blessed the world!

Key Verse

> "You will not be called Abram anymore. Your name will be Abraham, because I have made you a father of many nations. I will give you many children. Nations will come from you. And kings will come from you." (Genesis 17:5–6)

The Lord had said to Abram, "Leave your country ..."	Genesis 12:1
The Lord accepted Abram because he believed.	Genesis 15:6
Will a son be born to a man who is 100 years old?	Genesis 17:17
Abraham lived ... 175 years. He took his last breath ...	Genesis 25:7–8
Abraham believed because he had hope.	Romans 4:18
Abraham had faith. So he offered Isaac as a sacrifice.	Hebrews 11:17

Suggested Reading

Abraham and Lot.	Genesis 13–14
God makes a covenant with Abraham.	Genesis 17:1–22
God asks Abraham to sacrifice Isaac.	G enesis 22:1–19

Didjaknow?

Unbelievers used to say that many cities and empires talked about in the Bible never really existed. The Bible said Abraham's hometown was Ur. The scoffers said that there was no such place. But in 1922, archaeologist Leonard Woolley went to Iraq and excavated the city of Ur. "God is true, even though every human being is a liar" (Romans 3:4).

Adam and Eve

Adam and Eve were the first people God created. They lived in the Garden of Eden. One day Satan tempted Eve to eat a fruit that God said was forbidden. So she and Adam ate it. Suddenly they were afraid of God because they had sinned and disobeyed him. God sent them out of the Garden. Because Adam and Eve sinned, all people are born sinful.

Key Verse

"So God created man in his own likeness. He created him in the likeness of God. He created them as male and female." (Genesis 1:27)

Then the Lord God formed a man ...	Genesis 2:7
The Lord God put the man in the Garden of Eden ...	Genesis 2:15–17
The woman saw that the fruit of the tree was good to eat.	Genesis 3:6
... Lord God drove the man out of the Garden of Eden ...	Genesis 3:23

Admit

(See Confess)

Adultery

Adultery is having a physical relationship with someone you're not married to. We should love everyone, but some relationships are more important than others. The closest relationships are between husbands and wives. When people marry, they promise to be faithful and to physically love *only each other* for the rest of their lives. Adultery breaks this promise.

Key Verse

"Do not commit adultery." (Exodus 20:14)

A man who commits adultery has no sense.	Proverbs 6:32
Do not commit adultery.... Do not even look at a woman ...	Matthew 5:27–28
Does the law allow a man to divorce his wife?	Mark 10:2–9
God will judge the person who commits adultery.	Hebrews 13:4

We want to hear from you. Please send your comments about this book to us in care of the address below. Thank you.

Zonderkidz™

Grand Rapids, MI 49530
www.zonderkidz.com